GROWING HEALTHY ASIAN AMERICAN CHURCHES

EDITED BY
PETER CHA, S. STEVE KANG
AND HELEN LEE

D0168638

IVP Books

An imprint of InterVarsity Press
Downers Grove, Illinois

InterVarsity Press
P.O. Box 1400, Downers Grove, IL 60515-1426
World Wide Web: www.ivpress.com
E-mail: mail@ivpress.com

InterVarsity Press® is the book-publishing division of InterVarsity Christian Fellowship/USA®, a student movement active on campus at hundreds of universities, colleges and schools of nursing in the United States of America, and a member movement of the International Fellowship of Evangelical Students. For information about local and regional activities, write Public Relations Dept., InterVarsity Christian Fellowship/USA, 6400 Schroeder Rd., P.O. Box 7895, Madison, WI 53707-7895, or visit the IVCF website at <www.intervarsity.org>.

All Scripture quotations, unless otherwise indicated, are taken from the Holy Bible, Today's New International Version®. TNIV®. Copyright ©2001, 2005 by International Bible Society. Used by permission of Zondervan Publishing House. All rights reserved worldwide.

While all the stories of individuals and churches are drawn from actual people and circumstances, some names and identifying details have been changed to protect people's privacy.

Design: Cindy Kiple

ISBN-10: 0-8308-3325-0
ISBN-13: 978-0-8308-3325-2

Printed in the United States of America ∞

Library of Congress Cataloging-in-Publication Data

Growing healthy Asian American churches / edited by Peter Cha, Steve
  Kang and Helen Lee.
    p. cm.
  Includes bibliographical references.
  ISBN 0-8308-3325-0 (pbk.: alk. paper)
    1. Asian American churches. 2. Pastoral theology—United States.
  I. Cha, Peter. II. Kang, S. Steve. III. Lee, Helen.
  BR563.A82G76 2006
  277.308'308995—dc22

                                       2005027203

P	19	18	17	16	15	14	13	12	11	10	9	8	7	6	5	4	3	2	1
Y	19	18	17	16	15	14	13	12	11	10	09	08	07	06					

CONTENTS

Acknowledgments

THIS BOOK IS A COMMUNAL PROJECT. We would like to express our sincere gratitude to those who participated in writing this book, investing significant amounts of time in the midst of their busy ministry schedules. Thank you Paul Kim, Dihan Lee, Grace May, Soong-Chan Rah, Nancy Sugikawa, Steve Wong and Jonathan Wu. (See "Contributors and Catalyst Forum Participants" for information about these contributors and their ministries.) While each chapter was written by individuals, much of the content was provided by a group of Asian American Christian leaders who had gathered annually for three years (2002-2004); their insights and sharing of their rich congregational experiences made this book what it is. The forum participants included the above-mentioned writers, the three of us and David Gibbons, Ken Fong, Wayne Ogimachi, and Paul Tokunaga. It is important to emphasize that this book is not merely a collection of writings produced by different individuals; in many ways it was profoundly shaped by communal reflections that emerged from three years of engaging interactions enjoyed by a group of Asian American Christian workers.

We also want to thank the Catalyst Leadership Center for hosting, facilitating and funding the three-year forum gatherings, which resulted in the publication of this book. Since its inception in 1992, primarily through annual conferences and seminary-based leadership courses, Catalyst has been focusing on the task of forming Asian American Christian leaders; this book is another expression of Catalyst's ongoing commitment to this important task. We are also grateful to InterVarsity Press for taking a risk in publishing a book that can be perceived as an ethnic-specific work with a rather limited audience. We deeply appreciate their expression of care for the Asian American Christian community and their commitment to the diverse community of God's kingdom. Al Hsu, an associate editor of IVP, has been a wonderful guide and encourager. Given that book writing is a novel experience for many of us, Al's expertise and insights were truly God sent.

Finally, even as we offer this book that primarily focuses on the present and future of Asian American churches, we want to humbly acknowledge the invaluable contributions made by the forebears of Asian American faith and ministry, whether they are the early pioneers of the nineteenth century or many of our parents who established and served immigrant churches during the recent decades. Their legacy of faith is an important part of who we are and we gratefully acknowledge that.

Peter, Helen and Steve

INTRODUCTION

Growing Healthy Households of God

PETER CHA AND HELEN LEE

JOYCE LEE-JOHNSON SAT DUMBFOUNDED AT THE NEWS from the pulpit. Her pastor had just announced that he was planning to resign from his position as senior pastor of Great Neck Community Church, their one-hundred-member Asian American congregation—the latest in a long line of defections that the church had experienced in its ten-year history. Joyce, a thirty-three-year-old Korean-American pediatrician, her husband and fellow physician, Steve, and her toddler son, Justin, had chosen Great Neck largely because they felt warmly welcomed by this pastor; it also helped that there were other biracial families in the church.

But now, having been at the church for nearly two years, they were more aware of its inner workings and attuned to the forces that seemed to cause tension and strife in the congregation. One issue seemed to be a running debate over whether the church should be multiethnic rather than "Asian American." Another challenge was a continuing level of distrust that always seemed to exist between the lay leaders of the church and the congregation. Yet another challenge was finding a pastor who was able to live up to the high standards demanded by the members of the church, which was exhibited by this latest news. Over time, these issues had resulted in an erosion of

trust and enthusiasm within the congregation, and attendance and membership had slowly been waning. No pastor thus far had been able to manage
these and other conflicts within the church, resulting in the revolving door
of leaders throughout the church's history.

Joyce was not sure what to do. She and her husband had decided to come
back to church after having been away for many years; after Justin was born,
they had felt a growing conviction to return to their spiritual roots. Before
choosing Great Neck Community Church, they had visited numerous
churches, and many of the others seemed either too Caucasian or too Asian
for their tastes. But the church's constant leadership and attendance struggles caused her to worry about its future. She looked down at eighteen-
month-old Justin, oblivious to the instability swirling around him. In a few
years Christian education would be a critical element of what she would
need to see in a church, but at the current pace she was not sure how Great
Neck Community Church would be able to serve that need. She shared a
worried look with Steve, then held her son tight. Would they ever find a
church that was both a good fit *and* had the potential to survive?

■ ■ ■

On the surface it would seem that now is an ideal time to be an Asian
American Christian. In addition to the thousands of Asian immigrant
churches in America primarily serving the first generation, hundreds of
English-speaking Asian American and multiethnic churches have emerged in
cities all across America, with multitudes of pastors-to-be in training in key
evangelical seminaries. For example, at Gordon-Conwell Theological Seminary in Massachusetts, there was a 129 percent increase in Asian American
students between the early 1990s and the early 2000s, a statistic that is reflected in the enrollments of other key evangelical seminaries in the country.

And yet to accept these statistics at face value is to underestimate the
complexities facing the Asian American church today. In the 1990s the main
metaphor depicting the status of the Asian American church was "Silent Exodus," to explain the vast number of previously churched second-generation

Asian Americans who never returned to church once they left home for college. Today, these Asian American young people have options to consider because many more churches exist today to serve them than a decade ago. But these churches are not yet in a position to handle all the needs of their existing and potential members and attendees. Instead, the Asian American church finds itself at a critical point of transition—no longer nascent, but still struggling to reach its full potential. Congregations were launched in the late 1990s and early 2000s, largely by young pastors who did not have sufficient role models or support to help them with the daunting task of starting a church, and those congregations that have survived until today continue to experience growing pains from their inauspicious beginnings. Many of these churches struggle with leadership issues, with identifying and pursuing their mission and vision, with staffing problems, with organizational issues—and the list of challenges goes on and on.

As the children and grandchildren of first-generation Asian immigrants have begun to enter into adulthood and forge their own path in this country, so too have the emerging churches that focus on these later generations of largely American-born Asians. In some ways the current status of Asian American churches resembles the growth path of those they seek to serve: these congregations are breaking new ground as they develop their own identity and sense of calling. As these churches struggle with issues of leadership, spiritual maturity and a lack of resources or role models, they find themselves wrestling with the same questions that are often faced by the children of immigrants who are moving from childhood to adulthood: Who are we? What are we becoming? And what does the future hold for us?

"Where there is no vision, the people perish" (Prov 29:18 KJV) is a statement we frequently hear, particularly when going through periods marked by uncertainty and change. During the past two decades, as the Asian American community has faced such significant experiences of transition, pastors and lay leaders have responded by seeking to develop a clear ministry "vision" to lead and guide their congregations. Many leaders, however, have realized that they cannot develop an effective ministry vision in isolation, that one person or one congregation cannot clearly see the whole picture of what God is doing in our midst and what God's vision is for Asian American congregations.

A wise Christian leader once said that our God rarely shows one individual the whole vision of a given ministry, lest he or she might become prideful. Rather, God usually gives different pieces of that vision to different individuals, encouraging his children to come together to put together the whole picture of the ministry vision he provides. Indeed, when God's people gather to pray, listen and share with others their own pieces of the larger picture, like children working together on a jigsaw puzzle, what emerges is God's vision for the church.

Catalyst Leadership Center (originally named Katalyst) was launched fourteen years ago by a group of concerned Asian American pastors, partly to provide such a vision-making experience for Asian churches in North America. During the 1990s, Catalyst sponsored annual Asian-North American Christian Leadership conferences, bringing together more than five hundred Asian American pastors and lay leaders. In addition, between 1997 and 2001, partnering with seminaries such as Trinity Evangelical Divinity School and Talbot Theological Seminary, Catalyst also offered summer modular courses on Asian American Leadership Formation, inviting current seminarians as well as young pastors to enter into dialogue with more experienced pastoral leaders. Through these programs Catalyst provided a place where established and emerging Asian American Christian leaders could explore together their churches' current experiences and future direction. These events made it clear that our God is indeed powerfully at work among emerging Asian American congregations even as we experience many challenges and growing pains. These interactions also highlighted the need for us to carefully study and record how God is creatively shaping newly emerging Asian American congregations and what his vision might be for our churches, individually and collectively.

Perceiving such a need, Catalyst launched a three-year (2002-2004) leadership forum in which a group of Asian American Christian leaders from diverse ethnic, denominational and gender backgrounds gathered to share with one another their congregational stories and experiences, identifying certain challenges, opportunities and hopes. As the participants shared their congregational stories, what emerged was a clearer and hope-giving picture of what the Asian American church can be and is becoming. This book seeks to capture the vibrant picture of various congregations that emerged during our three-year experience of listening to one another and to our God.

In this book, we will focus on the theme of developing healthy Asian American congregations, exploring both "what we are becoming" and "what we are called to do," our identity as well as our mission. In doing so, we will use the biblical image of the household of God (Eph 2:19; 1 Tim 3:15; 1 Pet 2:5), an image that has not only deep theological meaning but also rich cultural nuances, particularly for Asian American Christians. So, what does a healthy Asian American household of God look like? What traits and qualities should characterize such a congregation? Indeed, how does a congregation become a healthy household of God?

Recent studies that have examined various congregations in the United States point out that each congregation has two forms of theology that guide and shape them. *Explicit* theology (proclaimed faith) is preached from the pulpit, taught in Sunday school classes and listed on the church's website as its statement of faith; it is what the congregation confesses as its belief. *Implicit* theology (practiced faith), on the other hand, is what the congregational leaders and members do when they gather together; it is a set of values and norms that guide how they make their decisions, relate to one another and allocate their resources. Studies point out that congregations grow most optimally when their explicit and implicit theologies are congruent with one another and thus reinforce one another. These studies indicate, however, most congregations fail to experience such an agreement between their two operating theologies. Furthermore, these studies find that between the two, implicit theology exerts greater influence in shaping the congregation and its members.

Paying close attention to both explicit and implicit theologies is especially critical for today's Asian American churches. On the one hand, given their specific context of ministry, Asian immigrant churches often function as ethnic cultural centers as well as spiritual communities. In such settings, while the church's explicit theology may be shaped by sound reflections on the Scriptures, the congregation's implicit theology can be easily molded by deeply rooted cultural values and norms, even by those elements that counter biblical teachings. On the other hand, as our society becomes more postmodern, the consistency between these two forms of theology becomes even more crucial. Today's young postmoderns, including Asian Americans, are searching and yearning for churches that are authentic and genuine, churches that earnestly seek to practice what they believe.

As we look at many Asian American congregations, we see that most of our congregations uphold biblically sound explicit theology, and we are grateful to our God for enabling these congregations to embrace and proclaim his truth faithfully. However, given our churches' unique relationship with our ethnic cultures, we need to prayerfully and critically examine the implicit theology of our congregations, making sure that what we do together reflects what we believe as God's people. It is our firm conviction that when our congregations' beliefs and actions mirror one another, when our churches are orthodox and engage in orthopraxis, our churches will continue to grow as healthy households of God.

In this book, then, we will explore a number of different Asian American congregations that are intentionally striving to grow as healthy households of God. In doing so we will particularly examine their implicit theology, exploring how their congregational values and practices, informed by their explicit theology, are contributing to the health of their church and the nurturing of their members. It is important to note that these churches were chosen not because they have "arrived," but because they are very intentionally striving to grow in this area of practicing what they believe. Furthermore, it is important to acknowledge that this book's aim is not to promote certain models, methods or strategies of ministry. The congregations presented in this book represent different ethnic backgrounds, theological traditions, geographic regions and are of different sizes; however, one thing they have in common is their strong desire to live out the biblical mandates and values in their own particular contexts of ministry. And as they do so, God's Spirit leads them through unique journeys of growth and transformation, further molding their identities and missions. It is our strong hope that this book will motivate and challenge you, whether you are a pastor, lay leader or a seminarian, to prayerfully think about the role you can play in helping your own congregation grow as a healthy household of God.

The book is divided into nine chapters, each focusing on a biblically informed value that we believe brings health to Asian American congregations. In discussing these values, each chapter will be framed around three components, *culture, gospel* and *leadership,* and it will examine (1) how Asian American culture affects the practice of the given value, both positively and negatively; (2) how the mandate of the gospel adds significance to that value as well as corrects our cultural practice of the value, and (3) how Asian American leaders exercise their leadership in shaping, affirming and practicing that value.

Asian Americans Christians often struggle with "toxic shame" that is largely produced by our cultural practices. In chapter one, "Grace-Filled Households," Nancy Sugikawa and Steve Wong address the question of how Asian American congregations face this issue of shame by living out a life of grace. And what does grace look like in Asian American congregations?

As people of the book, Asian American Christians are very committed to the authority of God's Word. However, given our own unique history, social location and mission field, Asian American congregations are developing different ways of engaging the Bible that allows them to be faithful to the Bible and be relevant to their particular context. In chapter two, "Truth-Embodying Households," Steve Kang addresses the question of how healthy congregations interpret, communicate and apply the Word.

Serving in young emerging churches, many Asian American pastors are facing the challenge of developing leadership principles and methods that might be effective in their context. In chapters three and four, both on healthy leaders and healthy households, Helen Lee examines the cultural roadblocks, biblical models and healthy practices and values from today's key Asian American church leaders.

Because many of our churches come from very tradition-bound cultures, continuity and conservation are emphasized. Yet for many emerging Asian American churches, change is inevitable and occurs often. Their ability to demonstrate flexibility in the face of change will greatly enhance their ability to minister effectively in their shifting environments. In chapter five, "Trusting Households: Openness to Change," Jonathan Wu examines what is involved in being open to change in a healthy manner.

For emerging Asian American congregations, evangelism has become more challenging than for Asian immigrant churches, due to cultural factors and forces such as the influence of postmodernism in our society. In chapter six, "Hospitable Households: Evangelism," Helen Lee examines how healthy Asian American congregations approach and practice their evangelism in such a way that they maintain authenticity while demonstrating relevance in our fast-changing world.

In many Asian ethnic congregations the intergenerational relationship between first-generation immigrants and American-born second-generation young people is the major flashpoint of conflict. However, congregations that are multiethnic also wrestle with generational issues as they seek to reach out to those who belong to older generations and to effectively nurture their own children in faith. Chapter seven, "Multigenerational Households," itself written by the intergenerational team of Paul Kim, Peter Cha and Dihan Lee, examines how healthy congregations intentionally nurture generational relationships and partnerships.

Given our Confucian heritage, gender relations in our culture and community are clearly marked by inequality and injustice. In chapter eight, "Gender Relations in Healthy Households," Grace May and Peter Cha explore how healthy Asian congregations choose to affirm women and their gifts, whether they are "complementarian" or "egalitarian" in their theological convictions. They will also demonstrate how the intentional practice of this value is critical to the overall health of these congregations.

Largely because of language and cultural barriers, Asian immigrant churches have not been actively involved in the ministry of mercy and justice in their own geographical communities. On the other hand, most English-speaking evangelical Asian American churches have also been inactive in this area, largely due to their conservative theology that discourages the church's social involvement. The churches that are participating in this book project, however, feel that the ministry of mercy and justice is an integral part of the kingdom ministry. In chapter nine, "Households of Mercy and Justice," Soong-Chan Rah will explore why these churches have passion in this area and how they are living out this passion.

It is our hope that all who read this book, whether a current or future church ministry practitioner, will find valuable insights and ideas to challenge, inspire and support their work in the critical mission field of Asian American young people. All the contributors of this book deeply desire to see more healthy Asian American churches start and grow, and we believe that the shared wisdom imparted in *Growing Healthy Asian American Churches* will help further the cause of the kingdom in these ethnic-specific and multiethnic communities.

1

GRACE-FILLED HOUSEHOLDS

NANCY SUGIKAWA AND STEVE WONG

A YOUNG CHINESE AMERICAN PASTOR HAS A brief affair with a woman at his church. His wife discloses his indiscretion to her close friend, the wife of one of the church elders. The church elder quickly confronts the pastor, who confesses everything and informs the elder that his wife plans on filing for divorce. The pastor is then told to take two weeks of "vacation" while the church elders debate his fate. He is quickly dismissed on the grounds that he has shamed the church and he can no longer be a godly role model for other church families. He and his wife are encouraged to move to a different part of the state and their departure is both sudden and secretive. The pastor is told not to communicate with anyone in the church, and the congregation is never told the reasons for his departure. After his move, numerous rumors feed the gossip circles, but no one speaks openly about what happened. The subject is not broached even by the few church people who keep in touch with the pastor and his wife. Forced to find a secular job, the now-divorced pastor slowly rebuilds his life. After a year he applies for another pastoral position but is told that the elders of his previous church would not give him a recommendation without commenting on why. He grows hurt and angry at both the church and God, and thoughts of reentering the pastorate or even attending another church leave him both bitter and broken.

Stories like this pastor's poured out during my [Nancy's] seminary years as I talked with my fellow students and those in full-time ministry. These stories were not just about pastors but about church members, especially those in the Asian American community, who were publicly shamed for their failures. They were about non-Christian friends who visited a church and were quickly reminded that they would "go to hell" if they didn't believe in God. These stories were about leaders who learned not to reveal their struggles with sexual purity, physical abuse or deep financial debts for fear of being judged.

Even as I was learning more and more about God's promises of forgiveness, restoration and grace, I wondered if I would be able to find, let alone help build, churches and ministries that embodied the true heart of God. My own ministry life had been filled with both hurtful as well as healing experiences, but these stories continued to burden my soul.

Why is it that churches are often places where God's grace is sadly absent? Is it possible for Christian leaders, and especially those in the Asian community who are devoted to God and his people, to be so filled with love that stories like these become few and far between? The key is building grace-based ministries that will transform not just our churches but our world.

WHAT IS GRACE?

The term *grace-filled* begs the question, What is *grace?* Popular definitions of *grace* include "seemingly effortless beauty or charm," "a temporary immunity or reprieve," "a short prayer of blessing or thanksgiving before a meal," or simply "goodwill." Biblically, the word *grace* comes from the Greek word *charis,* which can be defined as a "gift" or "God's divine favor" that is given freely to those he chooses. Grace is not deserved or owed and cannot be earned.

In his book *The Return of the Prodigal Son,* Henri Nouwen gives us a clear picture of grace by looking at Jesus' parable in Luke 15. It is the story about a young man who demands his inheritance from his father, then squanders it away until he must live like a beggar. He "comes to his senses" and realizes the righteousness of his father and decides to return to him and plead for mercy. Instead, his father greets him with open arms and pours out his love and generosity in abundance. Nouwen poignantly describes the painting by Rembrandt that depicts the meeting of father and son, and the elder brother who is displeased at his father's response.

The younger son, with shaved head and tattered clothes, bows broken and on his knees before his father who looks on him with love. The older son just looks on, distant, judging and prideful, believing that reward should come only to those who have worked hard and deserve it.

But grace is never deserved and cannot be earned. It is distinct from mercy, which can be defined as withholding punishment or *not* giving someone the retribution that they deserve. Grace on the other hand is giving someone something good that they do *not* deserve. Both grace and mercy are dependent solely on the giver, and are for the most part neither fair nor just.

And so this story might be more appropriately called "the parable of the generous father," who freely and abundantly gives both sons all that he has, regardless of how they treat him. It is a picture of grace and embodies the heart of our heavenly Father. This story provides this definition of grace: the outrageous generosity of God.

THE OUTRAGEOUS GENEROSITY OF GOD

Not long before Jesus went to the cross, he told a story about a vineyard owner who hired workers at various times of the day and paid those hired late in the day what he had agreed to pay those who had worked the entire day. Those who had worked the full day complained, but the employer answered, "Take your pay and go. I want to give the one who was hired last the same as I gave you. Don't I have the right to do what I want with my own money? Or are you envious because I am generous?" (Mt 20:14-15). God is generous—even when we are outraged by that generosity.

When we think of generosity we usually think of a favor that someone extends to another person. But God's outrageous generosity is more than a simple act of goodwill. It is an act of sacrifice, given at the expense of his justice. There was a cost to God's generosity, and it was paid by Jesus' death on the cross.

Christ's church is appointed by God to be the purveyor of his grace. This is the central characteristic of Christianity that sets it apart from other religions. Most religions are centered around what we have to do in order to gain God's favor or put ourselves in proper harmony with the universe. But the Christian God freely extends his unmerited favor even toward those who are his enemies (Rom 5:8). He shows them mercy, kindness and forgiveness, and in so doing transforms them into the image of his one and only beloved Son through the transforming work of his Spirit within them.

Christians give assent to this intellectually but often find it difficult to live as those who have partaken of this grace. Why? Our experience is that most evangelical church-goers (including the writers of this book and many of its readers) do their best to avoid looking like those who were hired last and are in need of God's generosity. We identify more closely with the workers who were hired at the beginning of the day and want to show that we have earned our keep. We pay lip service to God's grace, but we grumble at his outrageous generosity. Hence, we give the impression that God is really not that generous after all.

GRACE AND THE ASIAN AMERICAN CULTURE

The Asian American church in particular struggles with this most central gospel message, the message of the outrageously generous father of Luke 15 who runs out to meet a wasteful, shame-filled child and throws a party in celebration of his love for that child. Not only do we have difficulty identifying with the father's compulsion to celebrate, we have difficulty identifying with the younger son.

If we are church leaders, we probably rose to leadership by being like the older son: responsible and careful, keeping the family honor, not wasting the family resources. Honor and righteousness, living according to standards and expectations, are all of high value in Eastern cultures. Therefore, the older son can't understand how the father can be just and holy and still extend outrageous generosity to the younger son. Because the older son doesn't understand his father, he then misses out on even a small party for himself. His relationship to his father is ruled by fear, rather than infused with joy. Like his younger brother, he is also surprised and confused at his father's generosity. However, instead of responding in joy, he responds with bitterness.

The confusion of the older brother is our confusion. We are not used to seeing an Asian father throw off his hard-earned dignity and self-respect, to go running joyfully and lovingly toward an ungrateful child. To us, justice and generosity and holiness and grace seem mutually exclusive. Like the Pharisees and the teachers of the law, we tend to insist that people become perfect before entering the kingdom of God. In so doing, our churches can end up becoming places of dreary rule-keeping instead of places of true life and joy.

How does this happen? Greg Jao, in *Following Jesus Without Dishonoring Your Parents,* lists several Asian cultural elements that work against our acceptance of God's outrageous generosity: distant fathers, Confucian restraint and internalized shame.

A Korean senior pastor rebukes a younger pastor for missing morning prayer twice one week, challenging his devotion to God. He upholds as a better example of faithfulness another leader who works long hours and does everything he is told. A Chinese church elder scolds a pastor for not being spiritual enough because he has expressed his fear of failure or asked for a raise. A Japanese pastor has been having serious marital conflicts but urges his wife never to reveal their problems to anyone in the church.

The Asian church community is often taught to emphasize and reward hard work and external disciplines above mercy and internal transformation. Distant fathers and a heritage of emotional restraint have often robbed Asian families of ways to express familial affection as well as personal hurt or fear. Celebrations are often seen as frivolous compared to longsuffering and sacrifice.

Asians are taught to have a high regard for their elders and to maintain a proper public demeanor, but these values can often deter them from creating safe and authentic places to honestly confess their brokenness and failures.

How can the Asian church be transformed by the outrageous generosity of God? The story of the two brothers ends with the possibility of two choices. The older brother can continue to be resentful, even though the father has also reached out to him. Or he can begin to live in his father's outrageous generosity and join the lavish celebration. Imagine how different the older brother's life could be if he could see the kindness and generosity of his father. Imagine the transformation that could take place in his own heart if he could see that his father wants to use the family's abundant means to bless people, including himself. Rather than fearing him, the older brother would start enjoying life and relish being the son of an outrageously generous father. In 1 John 4:18 we read, "Perfect love drives out fear." That kind of love bears imitation, and that will have a transforming effect on us and on those around us.

A FOUNDATION FOR MINISTRY

I [Steve] was faced with the kind of dilemma every pastor hates. A couple that had been living together for thirteen years without being married had started to attend our church, Grace Community Covenant Church. The woman was a Korean American, the man a nominal Jew. She had grown up in church but left the church long ago. The man had no religious upbringing. They had met in college and had been together ever since. Their relationship was strong, having been tested even by her graduate studies and postdoctoral work. They had recently moved to Silicon Valley. They had come to realize that many of the people that they admired were Christians and decided that Christianity was worth checking out. They found our church through the Yellow Pages and were attracted to the fact that we were an Asian American church that was contemporary in worship style, so they started coming to our Alpha course (an introduction to the Christian faith) and made many friends. They loved being a part of the church community and were eagerly exploring what it means to be Christian. When was the right time to confront them with the fact that their lifestyle was displeasing to God?

There were several issues that crossed my mind as I mulled over the situation. The Bible clearly disapproves of a sexual relationship outside of marriage. If I did nothing, would the couple assume their living situation was acceptable or that Grace Community was a church that supported everyone's right to choose a comfortable lifestyle? Wouldn't other pastors and churches wonder about my staying true to the Word of God? They might think that I'd become "liberal" and had weakened in my convictions about the authority of the Bible. On top of that, we might start attracting people who approved of a less conservative approach to such situations. Others might say we were failing to maintain the purity of the church. We would risk being criticized by other evangelical churches. Or was there another way? Could we, as a church, truly live out what the Bible teaches about grace in our common life and in our interaction with this couple?

If grace is the outrageous generosity of God, then grace-based ministry is our service to God based on our experience of his generosity to us. Serving God entails serving others, both in the church and in our world. God's outrageous generosity is the basis for our service and it is also our message to the world. Everything that we do in God's name should be done in an outrageously generous way and with the offer of God's outrageous generosity.

A parable by Jesus illustrates this point, albeit in a negative way. In Matthew 18 Jesus tells of a servant who owes his king millions of dollars and is unable to repay the debt. The king has the right to seize all of the servant's assets and sell his family into slavery, but forgives the debt instead. When the servant is only steps away from the place where he has experienced this outrageous generosity, he comes across a person who owes him a few thousand dollars. Instead of passing on the generosity he has experienced, he uses the very law that the he had just escaped to throw the man into prison. Jesus' point is clear: we are to be like our generous heavenly Father or face the consequences of isolation and fear.

How is this kind of outrageous generosity worked out in the common life of a local church? How would such a community respond to the return of the younger son in Luke 15? The apostle Paul illustrates this in his letter to

Philemon. Philemon's slave, Onesimus, had probably stolen from Philemon and fled. Philemon had all of the weight of the law on his side. A runaway slave had no legal rights and if returned to the master could be beaten unmercifully. Onesimus had gone to Rome looking for anonymity to hide his status. In Rome, he came into contact with Paul and became a follower of Christ. Paul sent Onesimus back to Philemon with a letter that posits grace as the foundation for Philemon's future dealings with Onesimus.

Of course, we don't have slaves in our Asian American churches. But Paul's brief letter makes several key points about how people within church communities should treat each other. In the church our relationships with each other are based on our standing in Christ, not our previous merits or demerits. In other words, everything is now based on God's love for us. Love doesn't ignore our previous failings but has a vision of something greater for us. And that is how Paul asks Philemon to treat Onesimus, as someone who could have great value to him (Philem 11). In other words, Paul is telling Philemon to accept Onesimus as a brother in Christ, something that Paul had also told the Roman Christians (Rom 15:7).

In Christ, hierarchal relationships are dismissed. As Paul points out in another letter, "There is neither Jew nor Gentile, neither slave nor free, neither male nor female, for you are all one in Christ Jesus" (Gal 3:28). Race, class and gender are all distinctions on which social hierarchies had been and continue to be based today. They are distinctions over which the individual has no power, yet they are used to oppress or to hold onto power. Paul says there is a new hierarchy, an upside-down hierarchy of service. Within this hierarchy, Philemon owes Paul because he became a Christian through Paul's ministry (Philem 19).

Paul goes even further than asking Philemon to reinstate Onesimus into his household according to his previous position. He asks Philemon to treat Onesimus as if he were Paul (Philem 17) and to charge Paul with any money owed by Onesimus (v. 19). Some commentators feel that Paul is even implying that Philemon should be freed (v. 16). Again, Paul illustrates the principle of service, this time by putting his own reputation and even his pocketbook on the line to serve the best interests of Onesimus.

And that is the foundation for relationships in the church. We are to value everyone as a person loved by Christ, for whom Christ gave his life. We are to ignore previous distinctions that had been the basis for social hierarchy. That previous social structure is now turned upside down. Everyone is to serve the other. On this basis we are to look out for each others' needs (Phil 2:4), we are to encourage and build up each other (1 Thess 5:11).

All of this sounds quite reasonable to those of us who call ourselves evangelicals. But are we living it out? Philemon surely considered himself a good Christian. He had even had Paul as a house guest and Paul was expecting future hospitality from him (Philem 22). But when Onesimus showed up on his doorstep with a letter from Paul, it must have rocked Philemon's world. Paul was asking him to receive back this delinquent slave, and more, to accept him as a brother in Christ. Philemon was probably thinking, *But what about all of his previous misdeeds? You can't expect me to just overlook that!* But that's exactly what Paul was asking. And that was because Paul had once received the same acceptance and endorsement from a brother named Barnabas. Barnabas had asked the church to receive Paul as a brother, to rejoice in his salvation and to help him grow in his new relationship to Jesus, whom he had previously persecuted. The choice that faced the older brother in Luke 15 was the choice facing the church in Jerusalem and that now facing Philemon. Could he rejoice in the outrageous generosity of God the Father that was now extended to this formerly good-for-nothing slave and accept him now as a brother to be cared for and encouraged? Or would he demand some proof of a change of heart?

And so we have the same choice before us today. As Richard F. Lovelace puts it in *Dynamics of Spiritual Life,* do we believe that justification is by grace, but sanctification is by works? Or will we readily enter into relationship with anyone who responds to the call of God? That relationship is a means of grace, a way for God to do transforming work in everyone involved, both in those of us who identify with the older brother of Luke 15 as well as in those we would consider to be like the younger brother.

BUT WHAT ABOUT HOLINESS?

There is no doubt that grace-based ministry can pose a few challenges. It is risky and subjective. It takes place in the midst of values that are in constant tension with each other. Without a sensitive balance between grace and truth, grace-based ministry can often look like mere tolerance for sin. How do we extend grace without compromising personal holiness? How do we confront prideful or sinful behavior and still allow the Holy Spirit to work in his own time?

If we are true to God's Word, we find that there are consequences to sin, to disobedience to God's commands. We believe that the call to holiness is the way to life-giving freedom from sin and part of our commitment to relationship with a holy God. Refusal to turn from sin leads to the destruction of our soul and a hindering of the Holy Spirit's power in our lives.

So what is the difference between mere tolerance and approaching a situation with grace? Tolerance is taking the path of least resistance. Grace-based ministry seeks to know God's path toward holiness in any given situation. From a human perspective, it often seems that we are caught between indiscriminate acceptance and judgmental legalism. That was the seeming dilemma given to Jesus by the teachers of the law in John 8 when they presented to him a woman caught in adultery. But Jesus found a third way, the way of grace. It was not an easy way, and it took careful consideration and creativity. It didn't prevent Jesus from taking a clear stand on adultery. He named it as sin when he told the woman, "Go now and leave your life of sin." But he was more concerned with helping her toward God than enumerating the laws she'd broken.

Paul Hiebert, a missiologist, wrote a seminal article about the "centered-set" versus "bounded-set" approach to evangelism.[1] In bounded-set thinking, the focus is on getting nonbelievers to cross a line and enter into the set of believers. In centered-set thinking, the focus is on the trajectory of a person's life; that is, are they pointing toward or away from Christ? There is an understanding of redemption as a process.

There may be times when the boundaries are fuzzy. "Is a person a Christian or not?" To a centered-set thinker, that is not as important a question as asking, "Am I helping that person find Christ?" Grace-based ministry recognizes that people are in process, that life is a journey and that spirituality is about growth instead of accomplishments. Grace-based ministry responds by looking for ways to cooperate with what God is doing in a person's life, rather than worrying about reasons that might disqualify a person from God's kingdom.

Grace-based ministry is incarnational. In the incarnation God reached out to humankind. He had sent messenger angels. He had already communicated through creation and divinely inspired words. And he had even made brief appearances in our time and space. But he surpassed all other outreach media by becoming human, taking on our nature as well as our form. He reached out to us in the most personal way possible.

Personal outreach carries a lot of risk. The parable of the absentee vineyard owner who sent his son to collect his crop had a tragic ending: the tenant farmers killed the son (Mt 21:33-44). Jesus' crucifixion was the realization of this parable. But it also shows us that even when personal outreach seems futile, God can be working out a greater result. Emulating God's way of personal outreach carries risks: our stand on personal holiness may be misinterpreted, our personal space and time may be invaded; we may seem to be wasting our time. But if we rely on means other than personal relationship to communicate the gospel, we risk losing the heart of the gospel itself.

Engaging in such personal outreach may seem to necessitate risky contact with the world. But grace-based ministry believes that holiness, rather than unholiness, is contagious. In Jesus' day the Pharisees were very concerned with maintaining their holiness. To put a hedge around themselves, they would dissociate themselves from people who were too irreligious or had too unholy of a lifestyle. The concern with personal holiness was legitimate, but Jesus broke all their taboos by eating with the "sinners" everyone else avoided. He demonstrated the power of holiness by even touching corpses (e.g., the body of Jairus's dead daughter). In the same way, people may be surprised to find Christians involved in AIDS ministry, offering postabortion counseling or leading divorce recovery groups.

A pastor in the Asian American church is caught in immorality and is asked to step down from his position. Will he ever be able to serve in another pastorate again? A church elder is caught embezzling money from the treasury, although no civil suit is pursued. Can she ever be trusted in leadership again? Some Christians may be disturbed by the thought of an alcoholic, adulterer or exconvict sitting in the pew next to them in Sunday's worship service. But aren't these the very kinds of people we are hoping will walk through our doors to receive the hope and new life that Jesus brings? What does it take for the church to fully restore Christian leaders with God's grace and spirit of outrageous generosity, while maintaining holiness and a spirit of good stewardship?

The Chinese pastor at the beginning of this chapter found that it was easier to find grace and acceptance outside his Asian Christian community after his divorce. Another Japanese pastor, however, had a different experience. After his divorce, he resigned from his pastorate and began attending another church—one that was filled with grace and willing to accept him as he was. He took a job selling life insurance and slowly began engaging in a small group with both singles and families. He started serving behind the scenes with set-up and food preparation, and began to meet with the pastor for occasional counseling sessions. Both his small group leader and pastor saw his personal healing and growth as well as his faithfulness to his small group. After a year this former pastor was asked to co-lead his small group and eventually became a regular guest preacher at the church. Two years later a pastoral staff position became available and he was encouraged to take the position.

What was the difference between these two stories? One major difference was the role that relationships, or lack of them, played in the personal and ministry restoration of each pastor. Grace-filled relationships that offer opportunities for healing, trust-building and encouragement are key in the journey toward personal holiness.

Personal holiness is not a commodity to be acquired and protected. It is the expression of the life of God becoming more evident in us as we become more intimately acquainted with God, who is outrageously generous in his disposition toward us. That's why sanctification is a process: it is the result of a growing relationship with God, as opposed to the work of our wills. And that's why we don't need to fear that we will become contaminated by the world. When God's presence is growing in us, we begin to "contaminate" the world around us because "the one who is in you is greater than the one who is in the world" (1 Jn 4:4). As we grow in our love for God, "perfect love drives out fear" (1 Jn 4:18) and we, in turn, become outrageously generous toward the people that God loves and wants so much to redeem.

GRACE-FILLED ASIAN AMERICAN CHURCHES

So what does it look like when a church is operating by grace? Grace-based ministry is not a methodology to be imposed on a church. Rather, it is a foundation on which each local church can build its ministry. Each church has its own personality and cultural context that shapes its ministry. In order to explore how a church's ministry will build on the foundation of grace, it is necessary to examine both Asian American culture and Asian American church culture. And we recognize that "Asian American culture" is a problematic term. What we will attempt to do is to acknowledge some values that are held in common by the various Asian American cultural groups and look at the impact of these common values on churches that are led by Asian Americans, whether or not the churches themselves call themselves "Asian American." We'll then be able to see how grace-based ministry is built from these cultural materials.

ASIAN AMERICAN CULTURE

What are some values that are held in common by Asian American churches by virtue of their being influenced by Asian culture? From our experience we would suggest the following:

- hierarchy
- community and family
- education and achievement
- conformity and humility
- respect for tradition and elders

This is not an exhaustive list. Many studies have been done to better understand the nature of Asian cultures, particularly in contrast to the cultures of the West, and it isn't our intent to go over all of these. Many of our readers probably have their own lists of cultural values, undoubtedly based on their own ethnic background. But this simple list includes what we think are some of the core values held in common by most Asian cultures and which influence most Asian American local churches.[2]

A strong sense of hierarchy stems from a desire for order. When the individual is seen as the primary social unit, as in American culture, the social hierarchy is more fluid because the importance of individuals is seen to be dependent on their own merits and achievements. But in a society that is based on the collective identity of community or family, hierarchy gives the individual his or her identity. Achievement is a way for the individual to bring honor to the collective. Education is a means to achievement. The motivation for achievement comes not from the individual but from the collective. Conceding to the desires of the collective, rather than pushing a personal agenda, brings stability and growth for the collective, from which the individual derives identity. Elders are repositories of the wisdom of the collective. Traditions are expressions of the events that have shaped the collective.

Each of the values mentioned has helped the various Asian societies to survive for hundreds or even thousands of years. When Christ is "born" into each society, his presence may oppose, replace, complete or fulfill various aspects of the society's culture. The need for hierarchy, which springs from a desire for order and security, can be ultimately found in knowing the Creator and ordering our lives according to his design. Asian Americans who have found their source of identity in a collective of family or community can now find a more ultimate sense of community by being a part of God's family, and can find a greater sense of purpose by fulfilling their role in the body of Christ. The drive for education and achievement, which pushes many Asian Americans into joylessly living out the wishes of their parents and extended family, can be supplanted by the freedom of knowing that God loves us unconditionally. Individuals can find a joyful humility in serving others as Christ has served us. And the biblical emphasis on *kairos* events and on narrative affirms the Asian understanding of time as circular and the importance of tradition, as opposed to a Western valuing of progress and knowledge.

Much of the critique of core Asian values comes not so much from a biblical, grace-based perspective as from a Western (or more particularly American) perspective. This extrabiblical perspective can be seen from two historical periods. Some of the criticism came from the American fundamentalist Christian culture that nurtured many of the Asian American churches in the first half of the twentieth century. This culture was very American in its individualism, its distrust of "worldly" academic institutions, its valuing of achievement through individual effort (pulling oneself up by one's bootstraps) and its glorification of progress and newness. It's easy to see that the meeting of these two cultures would result in a great deal of conflict and that there would be a great deal of identity confusion on the part of Asian American Christians. Could they be truly Christian while holding cultural values that were so different from their mainstream American church brethren?

More recently, the American church-growth movement of the 1970s to the present has appealed to many young Asian American church leaders. And when they try to apply American church growth principles to their Asian American churches, they find resistance. No wonder. The church-growth movement is just a newer expression of the same ideals of American individualism that the fundamentalist church embodied. The churches that have been birthed by the church-growth movement may look very different from the fundamentalist churches of fifty years prior, but they still believe in the individual as the basic unit of society and arbiter of truth. They have a basic distrust of education. They believe in progress and newness as being inherently good: they just have a more contemporary standard for newness.

This is not to say that Asian cultural values are the ideal. Churches that have tried to build on a foundation of Asian cultural values rather than on a foundation of grace have found that their desire for order through hierarchy can evolve into tyranny, that the emphasis on the collective can smother individuals, that performance orientation can become meritocracy, that humility can become self-hatred, and that tradition can become a source of legalism. But a local Asian American church founded on grace can be a place where servant leadership helps to build a strong community that motivates each member to exercise her or his spiritual gifts in the power of the Spirit for the good of the whole and for the furthering of the gospel. Its worship will have a timeless quality because it is focused on the eternal God, but it will be relevant because it conveys the message of Christ's saving work for everyone. Such a church will find that responding to the outrageous generosity of God can have a uniquely Asian American expression.

And there is a flip side to the American Christian fundamentalist value system too. When built on grace, a church that is shaped by these values can be a place where individuals find their true value as those beloved by God. Such a church will keep itself holy, expressing the kind of life of the Holy Spirit that will make it very distinct from the world system. Yet they will seek to relate the timeless message of the gospel to society in relevant ways and do so with an entrepreneurial spirit. They will be motivated by the outrageous generosity of God toward themselves, which they seek to pass on to others in the spirit of Christ.

In Jesus' encounter with the Samaritan woman at the well in John 4, he never once brings up the issue of guilt and forgiveness. Instead, he draws out her story and shows her that God is the Father that accepts her and is even seeking her (Jn 4:23-24) in spite of her shameful past. Jesus enters into her story and in the process shows her that she can enter the ultimate story of God's work in the world. Unfortunately, the disciples return from buying lunch and scare the woman away, probably with disapproving looks, because Jesus, a Jewish man, is talking to a Samaritan woman. Jesus never gets to say to her, "Go now and leave your life of sin" as he does in John 8:11, but it doesn't matter. The woman is so excited by her newfound status as a daughter of God that she brings her entire village to hear Jesus.

Most of the churches in our experience are more like the disciples than like Jesus. We are more likely to drive people away with disapproving looks than to engage people and help them realize their spiritual thirst and find the source of living water. Our disapproving looks are based on the many standards that we've created to distinguish those who are serious about following God from those who aren't or are just trying to find a way to sneak in to heaven. God may see the heart, but we can only see the outward appearance (1 Sam 16:7), so we evaluate people according to what seem to be reasonable standards: spiritually oriented activities (like Bible reading and prayer) and lifestyle choices (like getting married).

I [Steve] was raised in a very conservative, fundamentalist Christian church. Our lifestyle choices were limited: no cards, no movies, no alcohol and so forth. In the same way, a good Christian was a person who engaged in the right spiritually oriented activities. (We would not have called them spiritual disciplines because that sounded too Catholic.) It was a badge of honor to have read the Bible all the way through, to carry a thick, leather-bound Bible, to be a "soul winner" and to have daily quiet times of Bible reading and prayer. The intent of these rules was good. Our church leaders wanted to keep us separate from the world and temptations that might lure our hearts away from God. And they wanted us to be involved in activities that helped us know God better and to express his life in our world. But the rules began to usurp the role of God. Paul tells the Galatians, "the law was put in charge to lead us to Christ" (Gal 3:24 NIV). But instead of bringing us to Christ, the rules became a standard for deciding who was in and who was out of the kingdom. The law became "the way, the truth, and the life" and no one was thought to come to the Father unless they followed the rules.

This substituting of things for personal relationship can be very subtle. For example, one would think that gratitude is a legitimate motivation for service, that we should serve God out of gratitude for his outrageous generosity. But in *Future Grace* John Piper shows us that this can become a way of introducing personal effort as a standard for righteousness. We outdo ourselves to show that we are more grateful than others, and we measure a person's spirituality by their works of gratitude. The Asian values of reciprocity and "face" become the basis for our service, not the outrageous generosity of God.

Instead, it is our trust in the character of God, based on his past dealings with us, that provides the only valid motivation for our service to God and others. We must trust that he will continue to be outrageously generous—even in the midst of our failures—before we can pass that understanding on to others. Then all of us will be on even ground. No one can claim to be more deserving of God's favor because he or she is more grateful. We must realize that God's grace is his very character, through which he embraces us even though we are ungrateful or undeserving.

As I pondered the situation of the unmarried couple that had been living together, I came to believe that our interaction with this couple needed to embody the truth, not as a judgment but as a corrective to shame-based religion that the woman had previously rejected in her Korean church upbringing. The fragrance of grace was beginning to draw them back to God and now was simply not the time to "lay down the law." And so the couple continued to participate in events at Grace Community. Through the Alpha course both decided to become followers of Jesus. The man had always wanted to be married, but the woman had put it off. The man and I were in a small group together and the topic of marriage had come up several times. Rather than warn him about "living in sin," I encouraged him to talk to the woman about getting married. We kept this as an item of prayer and eventually they asked me to perform their wedding.

This wedding was an affair to remember! When a couple has been to church all their lives, they may consider their wedding to be a private and personal affair. But this couple wanted everyone in the church to attend because this was their new family, and they wanted all of their unchurched friends to know the wonderful treasure they had found in God's grace. We all celebrated with them the work of the Holy Spirit in their lives, helping them to bring about a change in their lifestyle that reflected the process of transformation within and giving bold witness of that change to their unchurched friends.

They've continued to grow as Christians. They're committed to raising their infant daughter in the Christian faith. They act as liaisons in our church's partnership with our local Community Pregnancy Center and have organized other community service projects. The man has taken a new interest in his Jewish roots as he grows in his understanding of the place that the Jews have in God's redemptive purposes in the world. In fact, the woman jokes that since he's become a Christian her husband is now more Jewish than he's ever been, including observing Passover and hosting seders at their home. I have had the privilege of attending one. The story of this couple and of Jesus' encounter with the Samaritan woman illustrate grace-based ministry. *Ministry* is just a religious word for "service." So how do we serve each other, our community and our world? We do so on the basis of grace. Grace is God's redemptive activity in the world that has a flow, a story and a history. It's personal because it has an Author, someone giving it intentionality. It's also personal because it's about God's interactions with people. Ultimately, grace is about relationships and God's love for people.

THE POWER OF GRACE-BASED MINISTRY

How would a grace-based Asian American church respond to the young leader mentioned at the beginning of this chapter, the one who had failed in his marriage? Grace might mean that the elders work with the young pastor and his wife to help them find healing and reconciliation. Grace might mean financially supporting the pastor as he spent time in counseling. Grace might mean honest communication with the church congregation so that the whole faith community could support each other. Grace would work toward compassion, healing and growth in the lives of the pastor and his wife as well as in the congregation itself.

This kind of process may mean that the elders and other leaders would have to be honest about their own weaknesses, fears and failure to properly support and nurture that pastor. That too would be an extension of grace. God's outrageous generosity extends to everyone, including pastors. *Accountability* should not mean just another way of enforcing legalism. It should mean personal connection through which grace can flow, a connection both between individuals and between the individual and the community of faith.

Grace-based ministry is both an antidote to Asian culture and resonant with Asian culture. Grace-based ministry resonates with the emphasis on community and fitting in that are integral to Asian cultural institutions. The responsibility for changing people no longer rests solely on us as individuals, even if we are pastors. We are cooperating with what God is already doing in a person's life. We are free to participate in God's story of redemption rather than having to create a story from scratch each time we try to evangelize someone. What we are doing is building on the foundation of God's outrageous generosity with materials that come from our various cultural backgrounds. Without the foundation, a truly spiritual church cannot be built.

But on the foundation of grace, we can afford to be outrageously generous toward others, inviting them into God's family just as we ourselves, though completely undeserving, were also invited in. We will not be taking unnecessary risks but will be working in cooperation with God to redeem the world that he loves and for which he gave his Son. And in so doing, we will be the embodiment of God's outrageous generosity, living it out in our common life as well as offering it to others.

2

TRUTH-EMBODYING HOUSEHOLDS

S. STEVE KANG

AS A BASS GUITARIST DELIBERATELY PLAYED the last few notes of "Crown Him with Many Crowns," a well-choreographed Sunday worship service at Christ Community Church began without a glitch and sustained the interest and participation of the congregation, lasting exactly one hour and fifteen minutes from the opening praise to the measured words of benediction. The worship service was creative, intentional and heartwarming, the fruit of hard work and consistent weekly planning and rehearsing by several committed members of the worship team. The congregation has come to expect such excellence from this upscale Asian American church.

Christ Community was started nine years ago by a group of Asian American leaders who wanted to reach out to unchurched Asian Americans in a major American city that has seen an exponential growth of various segments of this population in recent years. From the inception of the church to the present, the vision of Christ Community Church has been to be a seeker-sensitive, culturally relevant, gender-affirming, justice-focused, mission-minded, intentionally (yet subtly) Asian American and Bible-believing church. Over time, the church has steadily grown in numbers and budget, and has become more multiethnic, multicultural and intergenerational. It appears that Christ Community Church has all the makings of becoming a model for the Asian American church.

As the church prepared for its tenth-anniversary celebration, its leadership decided to document the impact the church has had on the members of the congregation. As expected, many positive stories of appreciation were told. However, to the leaders' surprise, many in the congregation expressed feelings of burnout, spiritual stagnation and yearnings for more authentic relationships with God and others in the church community. The church leadership quickly formed a task force, including several lay leaders and a couple of outside consultants.

After three months of extensive research, the task force came back with a report. There were three crucial findings: (1) lay leaders felt that their Christian identities revolved around how much of their spiritual gifts and time they could give to the church, causing many people to feel inadequate to serve in a church that seemed to demand excellence in all aspects; (2) some observed that, for the sake of being culturally relevant, the church had assimilated too readily and uncritically at times to the ever-changing milieus of both mainstream culture and "successful" megachurches; (3) many in the church expressed their yearning for wholeness, an integration and rootedness of various aspects of their lives in the Word of God and church life. The report brought the whole congregation to commit to allowing God's truth to pervade every aspect of church life, continuing to *realize* itself as a community where God's truth and grace permeate every aspect of the congregation as well as each member.

In recent years there have been many Asian American church plants, not unlike Christ Community Church, springing up in major cities across the United States. By and large these churches are well-conceived. They are Bible-centered, culturally relevant, lay-driven and outreach-focused. These churches are highly energetic and multifaceted, untiringly meeting the needs of the congregation and its target group. However, as these churches ponder the trajectory of the church, many realize that they have been running on empty, often striving for quantitative results that indicate the outward growth of the church. While many of these churches have been true to their mission, it is incumbent for them to reexamine how well they have been embodying the truth of God in every aspect of community life. As discussed in chapter one, God's grace is not merely a license to abuse God-given freedom or to overlook the glaring disobedience of an individual or a congregation. God's grace is his saving work for Christians, which subsequently stimulates us to respond to his saving work through the power and gifts that he faithfully provides for the church (1 Cor 15:10). Thus if grace-based ministry is to continue to claim God's grace in action, it must strive to grow as a community that continues to discover and embody the truth of God through and through. Perhaps the church needs to ask itself a salient question: Has the truth of God permeated and does it continue to permeate the very fabric of the Asian American church so much so that it is well on its way to becoming an extension of God's truth and grace within and beyond the church in God's kingdom?

EMBODYING TRUTH AS A WAY OF LIFE

From its inception the church of Jesus Christ has engaged in the cultivation of a lifelong *habitus*[1] toward the image of Jesus Christ. Through the centuries this cultivation process has taken certain forms, engaging the community of believers in faithful pursuit of the knowledge of God and creation and the cultivation of self. Fostering such a lifelong quest for each generation of believers has required a profound interplay of all human dimensions—cognitive, affective, volitional and behavioral.

The past two decades have seen renewed attempts by the Protestant church, under the banner of spiritual formation, to cultivate the *habitus Christi* in an ever-changing and fragmented world. Recently, much has been written and many programs have been developed on the nature and practice of spiritual formation, and these have permeated the fabric of the American church. Observing the proliferation of such a movement, however, Donald Bloesch has warned that this phenomenon seems to be drifting away from the theological commitments of evangelicalism. Commenting on the growing fissure between spirituality and theology, Bloesch reminds us:

Spirituality refers to living out our lives in relation to the Eternal, appropriating redeeming grace in trust and obedience. If revelation involved only objective truths, the religious affections would be quenched and the religious yearning suppressed. Christians are spiritual, as well as rational, beings, and this means being in contact with the Spirit of God as well as with truths revealed by God.[2]

In response to this caution there have been some encouraging signs in the past two decades or so; some evangelical leaders have been rediscovering the theological dimension of Christianity within their own faith communities.[3] They have urged the church to reconceptualize its theological inquiry as a spiritual exercise for the service of the church. For instance, Ellen Charry, who teaches theology at Princeton Theological Seminary, maintains that theological inquiry should be a "religious practice in which God's grace may reshape the seeker. . . . Studying theology is riskier than studying chemistry because its goal is the nourishment and transformation of the soul."[4] In other words, Christian theology and spirituality share a common goal of soul (trans)formation into the image of Jesus Christ, so that "Christian beliefs and practices can nurture people intellectually, morally, and psychologically in the course of everyday life and work."[5]

Seen in this light, it seems that the vision of the church in general and the Asian American church in particular as the truth-embodying community is to engage in the continual formation as the people of God—as a chosen people, a royal priesthood, a holy nation, a people belonging to God forever (1 Pet 2:9)—through Jesus Christ, the living Word, who has revealed and continues to reveal himself through the Bible, the written Word, and the Holy Spirit. In turn, this vision of the church ought to guide Asian American Christians' entire lives.

CAN THE ASIAN AMERICAN CHURCH REALLY BE A TRUTH-EMBODYING COMMUNITY?

Is there a need for ethnic-specific ministries? Where do you find ethnic-specific ministries in the Bible? Isn't the Asian American church phenomenon a direct result of multiculturalism in ever-secularizing America? Doesn't the Asian American church inevitably end up focusing more on the culture than the truth of the Bible? Those who are involved in Asian American ministry often have been confronted with such questions by well-meaning Christians, exposing their displeasure about the existence of the Asian American church.

From the founding of the United States the Christian church, both Protestant and Catholic, has been highly ethnic specific in its formation and maintenance—until recent years. Much of American denominationalism can easily be traced back to the persistence of ethnic church enclaves. It is ironic that while much-celebrated theories of homogeneous unit principle and contextualization have been the dominant partners in much of the world missions strategies, such strategies have been largely looked down on as ways to accommodate the spiritual needs of the burgeoning population of recent immigrants and their subsequent generations. To the liberal wing of American Protestantism, ethnic-specific churches have been, by and large, seen as a nuisance to its movement, often treated as inevitable consequences of secular multiculturalism at best. On the other hand, to the conservatives, ethnic-specific churches are welcomed so long as these churches come under the care of their denominational leadership, boosting their numerical growth and enlarging their sphere of influence.

Yet perhaps the most significant challenge that ethnic-specific ministries encounter from conservatives is the cloud of suspicion—can they be genuinely Bible-believing churches without being compromised by their cultural trappings? Here lies the dilemma for ethnic-specific churches, particularly Asian American churches. American evangelicalism urges Asian American churches to keep the so-called historical Christian faith apart from their own cultural heritages. Yet Asian American churches are often looked on in the Asian American community as a place that accelerates acculturation into mainstream America, acquiescing their own cultural heritages in the process. In such milieus, can the Asian American church function as a truth-embodying community?

THE LIFE IN A TRUTH-EMBODYING COMMUNITY

Christian identity and sacraments. The Asian American church as a truth-embodying community understands that the triune God graciously elected God the Son, Jesus Christ, through whom God's people have been chosen from before the foundation of the world (Eph 1:4). That election was fully realized when Jesus Christ broke through the human plane to live among us, to die and to rise again. At that Christ event we were given the promised Holy Spirit, through whom we receive the gift of faith, and it is only through the gift of faith that we can wholeheartedly affirm that Jesus Christ is the head of the church. For this reason the church can be described as the space and time where God's chosen people affirm their new life in Jesus Christ through worship, instruction, fellowship and expression. In this sense the church may be construed as the household of God, through which God continues to manifest his glory on earth. As the household of God, the church seeks to faithfully respond to the gracious triune God by hearing and obeying the truth of God in Jesus Christ through the Holy Spirit and the written Word.

However, the present-day Western Protestant church has largely individualized and privatized the depth of God's election of his *people* in Jesus Christ. The modern church has tended to construe the *individual* elected by God as the basic unit that *makes up* the church. As a corollary, Christians are taught to find their self-identity and God's will for their personal lives as individuals. In this chapter's opening story, the members of Christ Community Church were feeling pressured to perform for the church, based on their individual talents. This resulted in little spiritual depth and even burnout. This inordinate emphasis on the individualization of Christian identity and life produces Christians who feel useless because their faith has become privatized and their spiritual life compartmentalized, reshaping the church as a voluntary organization where individual Christians come together to meet their own unmet needs in a utilitarian sense.

Yet the church is *not* merely a voluntary gathering of like-minded people with similar interests—as in a homogeneous unit. The church is the earthly embodiment of the risen Christ, the truth-embodying community in time and space, dwelling and lingering in God's kingdom. The truth-embodying community is exhorted to function as a mutually formative community, continually invoking the Holy Spirit's transforming work in order for it to realize God's kingdom. To rectify the torrential movement toward individualized and privatized faith, the truth-embodying community must submit to the triune God's loving intention to proclaim Jesus Christ to the whole world and to summon humankind to faith in him.

Having grown up in a more collective immigrant culture as second-generation Asian Americans (or having been immersed in a collective Asian American culture as third, fourth, or even fifth-generation Asian Americans), Asian American Christians can readily understand how we Christians have been chosen by the triune God as a collective body from the eternity past in Jesus Christ. In this light we affirm that it is not solitary individuals who freely choose to believe God that make up the church, rather it is the gracious God who has chosen the collective body of Christ, and here we find our identity as the persons who belong to the household of God. We observe many Asian Americans who refer commonly to one another as sisters, brothers, aunts and uncles. While such a practice can be found in more collective cultures in general, and in Asian and Asian American cultures in particular, Asian American Christians instinctively understand that in Christ we are genuinely sisters, brothers, aunts and uncles in the household of God! In the Asian American church, such a truth is not merely affirmed cognitively as a theological proposition or an unreflective cultural practice as in syncretism, but it takes on the full meaning in the life of the community as an essential framework of its habitus. Asian American Christians readily envision how the corporate hearing of the Word and faithful obedience to the Word coalesce in all the dimensions of the church, namely teaching, fellowship, breaking of bread and prayer.

For instance, in deciding how they should celebrate the Lord's Supper an Asian American church in the Midwest decided to examine in a fresh way how they could appropriately bring together in their corporate worship the motif of the household of God and the Christ event. After carefully studying the meaning and practices of Communion, they decided to hold Communion based on the Scots' understanding and practice, wherein the bread and wine are to be received sitting around a table. The Scots' form of Communion, which is heavily influenced by the spirit of the Reformation, is primarily based on the objection that taking Communion while kneeling would not only encourage idolatry and superstition but be construed as the gesture of beggars or suppliants, who question hopelessly whether they will be received by God or not. Instead, the Scots decided that the practice must declare the joyful significance of the Supper, affirming that we are sons and daughters of God invited by our glorious King to his own table. The church appropriated this tradition not merely to follow the Scots' form but to declare that we are indeed the children of God, those called to be the household of God, and we affirm our fellowship, praying with and singing to one another precisely because of what Jesus Christ has done for us.

In this manner, healthy Asian American churches are rediscovering the meaning and function of sacraments in the life of the church. Steve Wong, pastor of Grace Community Covenant Church, believes that the sacrament of baptism has fallen into disrepute in the American evangelical church in recent years due to the fight over the mode of baptism, thus losing its salient and formative role in shaping the household of God. As a pastor he has observed many Asian American Christians who, through experiences in various denominations, were confused about the mode of baptism, resulting in confusion about embracing the significance of the sacrament. So his church leadership decided to teach about the various meanings and practices of baptism to the whole congregation. However, before teaching the congregation about baptism, Pastor Wong embarked on a thorough study of baptism for himself in order to provide the mosaic of a balanced and thorough understanding for his congregation. Having grown up in a more baptistic tradition and espousing its view of baptism, he committed himself to learning with respect rather than judgment the Reformed understanding and practice of baptism from the founders of the Reformed tradition of the church, tracing the topic all the way from John Calvin's *Institutes of the Christian Religion* to some contemporary Reformed theologians.

For his church the main purpose of such teaching was to let the congregation understand the importance of baptism in the life of the household of God through the context of the historic and global church. They wanted the baptized individual to declare in public that he or she is now a member of the household of God, and for the household of God to welcome and commit itself to nurture the baptized as a brother or sister in Christ. In the case of infant baptism and infant dedication, both the parents of the infant *and* the congregation commit themselves to raising the infant in the household of God and to asking God to grant his mercy on the child. In sum, healthy Asian American churches believe that they are to faithfully allow the full meaning and the practice of the sacraments of the church to strengthen, nourish and form the life of the church as the truth-embodying community.

Theological reflection in the truth-embodying community. Again, healthy Asian American churches understand that the Word of God, who is very God himself, has graciously given the written Word of God, the Bible, and that it continues to become the Word of God to us in our meditation, proclamation and obedience through the illumination of the Holy Spirit. When Jesus said, "Then you will know the truth, and the truth will set you free" (Jn 8:32), Jesus was not referring to a set of esoteric propositions conceptualized by human beings. Instead, Jesus Christ, the God-man, is referring to himself as the truth par excellence, through whom we can approach God the Father and have life to the fullest (Jn 14:6; 10:10). It is *this* Jesus who invites us to join in the eternal communion with the triune God who holds everything together in Jesus Christ (Col 1:17).

We must be careful that our community does not construe the Bible as a "history-like" narrative to be merely subsumed into the community's already existing narrative of truths and traditions. Instead, the truth-embodying community continues to receive Jesus Christ, who continues to reveal himself through the indwelling Holy Spirit and the Bible. Through the living and written Word and the power of the Holy Spirit, the community boldly affirms and realizes itself as the truth-embodying community that God has called it to be. Thus the truth-embodying community is nothing less than the God-initiated community in which the life, death and resurrection of Jesus Christ are celebrated and continue to shape the way of life of its people through the power of the Holy Spirit. All of this is attested in the Bible, the written Word of God.

It is one thing, however, to cognitively affirm the descriptions of the truth-embodying community and quite another to actually live out the reality of such community. Faced with such a challenge, healthy Asian American churches must continually ask themselves whether they have intentionally allowed the Word of God, through the work of the Holy Spirit, to shape the identity, life and trajectory of the truth-embodying community. Peter Cha, who teaches at Trinity Evangelical Divinity School, has observed a disturbing trend among Asian American pastors and leaders in the country. He asserts that many Asian American pastors and leaders trained in leading evangelical seminaries think that

> when they graduate from seminary, they're done with *theological* education. They then go into ministry thinking that theology is to be left in a seminary for theologians to write about and teach. They think they are done with theology—they've passed their exams and their ordination exam—and now theology doesn't matter. It's almost the end of theological reflections. And it concerns me in that churches are being guided by theologically unreflective pastors and leaders.

What Cha is concerned about is not unrelated to the problem in evangelical seminaries in the United States today, which demands homogeneous thinking with little divergence from one line of thought, the modernistic Western European approach. But in most other spheres of life the United States has experienced great diversity—a rapidly expanding and influential pluralism. This is not merely observed in the multiplicity of people of ethnic and racial backgrounds but also among genders, classes, generations, ideologies, and regional distinctives, just to name a few. Faced with the complexity of this era, the church must grapple with what and how God might have his people respond as the truth-embodying community. Too often when Asian American students attend evangelical seminaries, they are asked, often unintentionally, to put away their rich cultural heritages and practices in favor of the dominant tradition in American evangelicalism. No wonder that many Asian American pastors and leaders are often ill-equipped to minister in the Asian American church. They often comply with the mainstream American way of doing church by unreflectively borrowing from either successful megachurches or notable mainstream Christian thinkers who advocate some sort of one-size-fits-all teaching for all contexts and all times. Thus the Asian American pastors struggle to understand the particular place and role the Asian American church is called to fulfill in God's kingdom. On the other side of the spectrum are those Asian American pastors and leaders who are highly critical of those Asian American churches that borrow from the successful American evangelical models and methods that have nothing indigenously Asian American about them.

In responding to such a quandary, Wayne Ogimachi, founding pastor of Lighthouse Christian Church in Seattle, has skillfully guided his church as a truth-embodying community. He says that he does not necessarily assume that just because an Asian American church adopts certain models of ministry or materials from another successful church that the Asian American church did so uncritically or without regard to its own context. Ogimachi says:

> When I was a pastor, anytime I'd read a book, go to a conference, hear a message, I'd try to be discerning and say, what does this mean to me and my congregants? Does it have any application to my life or my ministry setting? . . . I appreciate a biblical pastor, who with whatever he'll hear or read, will say, "how does this square with the Bible?" I also want to see and hear how that model or idea resonates with our understanding of the Bible. We wouldn't adopt something just because some other church did and it worked for them.

For instance, when his church was deciding to adopt a highly successful program that was not inherently Asian American, Pastor Ogimachi and the leaders of the church carefully studied the context and purpose of the program, and tried to discern whether the program was theologically sound and potentially life-giving to the congregation. Upon its adoption, the leaders carefully planned how, in light of the church's vision, the program would be conveyed to the congregation. They also studied how to reinforce the program theologically and how to contextualize to their particular circumstances.

David Gibbons, lead pastor of NewSong Church, is widely considered a risk-taking, innovative pastor among Asian American church leaders. However, considering his childhood upbringing and education, it's surprising that Gibbons was called to be such a pastor. His fundamentalist background would suggest that he would be dogmatically committed to what he believes to be true. Yet Gibbons has always been sensitive to God's leading and serious about studying the Bible with an open heart. Gibbons has been serious about reexamining the Bible on key issues, such as women in ministry and social justice, spending significant time with key conversation partners who have devoted much study and have exercised graciousness and truth-embodying leadership on those issues within their spheres of influence.

Theologizing as participating in the kingdom drama. When we affirm our belief in the holy catholic church and the communion of saints, we are in fact affirming our fellowship with the mosaic of fellow Christians—all those who came before us and those of the present world—who call and have called on the name of Jesus Christ. The communion of saints, of course, is only possible because of our crucified and resurrected Jesus Christ, who has brought us into eternal communion with the triune God. And communion with God requires that the church *realizes* itself—by the church's faithful reading of and reflection on the Bible now and throughout history—as a part of the unfolding of God's gracious redemptive drama.

As a truth-embodying community the Asian American church is well poised to enter into the biblical drama by realistically envisioning the communion with fellow saints in the communities of the global church past, present and future. We see that God's sovereign calling of his people, which began with the promise of Abraham, has continued throughout God's redemptive history and continues now with people of every nation and color. We affirm that there is fundamentally no historical difference between the community in which Scripture was introduced and the church that presently seeks to understand the same Scripture. These are the *same* community theologically and spiritually, even if not socially and politically.

The Asian American church can readily envision the church of Jesus Christ as a mosaic that consists of the Christians of the past, present and future from all parts of the world. While a major problem with much modern biblical interpretation has been the assumption that one, historically identical, universal church does not exist, the Asian American church affirms that the past and present do not need to be bridged *before* understanding can begin; past and present are already mediated by the continuity of the Holy Spirit through the community's language and discourse.

Ogimachi warns about how a reification of theology can result in stunted growth among the people in the church. He says:

> One of the dangers we face . . . is that we tend to focus only on the orthodoxy. There's a danger especially in Asian American cultures' emphasis on knowledge. We think, "If I say the right things, I am a mature Christian." But, if it doesn't transform the heart and move beyond, what's the point?

He believes that Asian Americans are simply reflecting the high value we put in "bookish" learning, equating biblical and theological knowledge as the measure of Christian maturity. Ogimachi continues, "I've seen too many congregations that are solidly committed to right doctrine, doctrinal purity. They know all the doctrine, but it makes no difference in their practical lives. If their marriages are a wreck, or whatever the challenges happen to be, the right doctrine has no impact in their lives. How do we get past this bifurcation?"

In a similar vein, Wong asserts that, for pastors and leaders of the church, the opposite of truth-embodying is leadership laziness. He says:

> Pastoral laziness says, 'Well, it's been done by my denomination and
> I'll do it, . . . or it's been done by such and such, so I will just do it.'
> This is critical. . . . We can't just adopt wholesale things simply be-
> cause they're being done by somebody else. We're going to critically,
> reflectively study the Bible, go back to our historical roots, whatever it
> takes, so that we can preach and model with integrity.

As a case in point, Soong-Chan Rah, pastor of the Cambridge Community Fellowship Church, has been keen on fighting against the typical American Protestant tendency to bifurcate various Christian issues, resulting in
further divisions within the already fragmented church of Jesus Christ. What
is even worse is that seminary-trained Asian American pastors and leaders,
influenced by their seminary education, often fall into the same trap by unreflectively aligning themselves and their churches along the existing dividing lines. Pastor Rah is quick to point out that many Asian American pastors,
trained in more conservative seminaries, have bought into the fact that their
churches are to hold on to the "gospel"—knowing right doctrine and evangelizing the lost—as opposed to living out the "social gospel"—engaging in
social justice issues and social action. He bemoans the fact that Asian American churches are influenced by some of the unfortunate bifurcations that
are the direct results of sociohistorical conditions in America (e.g., the mod-
ernist-fundamentalist controversy of the early twentieth century). Being
cognizant of such bifurcations, Cambridge Community Fellowship Church
has tirelessly sought to reflectively live out the fullness of the gospel of Jesus
Christ, where proclamation and praxis are of the same gospel. Rah has included among his mentors African American pastors who have exemplified
the integration of orthodoxy and orthopraxy. At Cambridge Community
Fellowship Church, such an integration has taken deep root and has become
the very fabric of every facet of the church's ministry.

Furthermore, the concern for the bifurcation does not stop at the liberal-
conservative Christian traditions. Healthy Asian American churches also

will reexamine various divisive issues that exist within the conservative evangelical tradition. A growing number of Asian American pastors and leaders are wary of restricting Christian fellowship based on unnecessary dividing walls: the age of the earth; the mode of baptism; the charismatic gifts; women in ministry; and generational, ethnic, racial and class differences, just to name a few. They are convinced that such dividing walls have often been erected by a few ideologues and that the church seldom critically assesses those divisive issues as a truth-embodying community. Having either experienced or observed painful church splits, many of today's Asian American churches are much more careful in addressing some of the thorny and potentially divisive issues in the contemporary church in America.

The manner in which an Asian American church in the Midwest went about addressing the women in ministry issue is instructive. The church decided to examine together the potentially divisive issue by inviting a Bible scholar who had studied the areas of gender issues and hermeneutics to give an all-day workshop. Their intention was not to have him give his scholarly opinion on women in ministry, but to provide the congregation with some theological tools to deal with the issue and to show how the process of coming to a conclusion on such a theological issue should evolve. After a joint congregational exercise, the church drafted a theological *and* practical paper on the issue. This exercise not only settled the particular issue for this congregation but also offered them a way to think about various church and community issues theologically. When church leaders take seriously the indwelling Holy Spirit and the priesthood of all believers, such a process of corporate learning and deliberation can become a reality in a truth-embodying community.

Bible reading in the truth-embodying community. As a concrete practice of the truth-embodying community, the Asian American church needs to continually reflect on whether it intentionally allows the Word of God to be its master. As contemporary readers of the Bible, we are accustomed to engaging the Bible with scientific procedures (e.g., observation, interpretation and application) to decipher exactly what God intended. In the process we have inadvertently convinced ourselves that we are able to *master* the Bible, the Word of God. What a tragedy! The written Word of God is not given to the church to be mastered; rather the Word of God is the master that ushers us into the kingdom reality!

Over the years I have observed two diverging approaches by Asian American pastors and leaders in terms of preaching the Bible. One approach is based on inductive study of a given Bible text, which results in a main proposition and three supporting subpropositions. The other approach is a reaction against the rather formulaic preaching of the first approach. This approach asserts that preaching should be done narratively, basically retelling the stories of the Bible to contemporary hearers. I see the latter gaining momentum by more prominent Asian American pastors. Ken Fong, senior pastor of Evergreen Baptist Church in Los Angeles, believes that more and more people are drawn to stories rather than precepts: stories possess the potential for "childlike people to enter into them." He continues, "Whenever there is a coalescing of our own stories with God's there is always the potential for a mysterious melting of even the hardest of hearts." He even goes so far as to say that "doctrinal precepts are important, but they can come later. First we must believe that there is tremendous transformational power in (the) story."[6]

Indeed, the abuse of the first approach, making every genre of the Bible fit neatly into a prescribed formula, must be carefully critiqued in teaching and preaching situations. However, the overemphasis on the power and place of stories also must be carefully nuanced. While it is true that people all over the world and throughout history, Asian Americans included, have relished stories in general, what must be emphasized in our teaching and preaching of the Bible is God's redemptive drama, the grand narrative in which the biblical stories and our own come together. In this light, Bible reading in the Asian American church should be based on faithful study of the Bible—utilizing various approaches to reading the Bible that have been practiced throughout the church—in order to envision the historical unfolding of the grand narrative that the triune God has revealed to the historic church. Moreover, the Asian American church must be keen on listening to how the Bible is read by the church all around the globe, in order to envision the breadth of the grand narrative that can never be fully captured by a church in a particular time and space. Kevin Vanhoozer, who teaches theology at Trinity Evangelical Divinity School, asserts:

> There is a single meaning in the text, but it is so rich that we may need the insights of a variety of individual and cultural perspectives fully to do it justice . . . to attest to the abundance of meaning. . . . The single correct meaning may only come to light through multicultural interpretation.

He continues:

> The Holy Spirit leads the Church, in all its cultural and racial variety, into a deeper appreciation of the one true interpretation of the Scriptures. This should not surprise us, for the event of Jesus Christ itself takes all four gospels together to articulate it. This is a "Pentecostal plurality," as it were, which believes that the objective textual meaning is best approximated by a diversity of reading contexts and communities.[7]

Moreover, the Bible is not just another book that needs to be mastered by ordinary readers or even by the guild of modern exegetes. The truth-embodying community should not succumb to modern scientific and historicist assumptions, which inevitably reduce the text to its historical sense, but should read the Bible as the gracious unfolding of the triune God's drama for his people. For instance, in the preaching and teaching ministries of the Asian American church, there should be much more conscious effort made in bridging *both* the Old and New Testaments. Also the church's teaching and preaching of the Bible could be more attuned to the seasons of the Christian calendar, which is basically structured around God's redemptive story of his people. This would facilitate God's people living more consciously in accordance with the redemptive plan and thus entering, lingering and dwelling more fully in the biblical reality.

Last, we need to realize that reading the Bible impartially or in light of its sociohistorical embeddedness is not a guarantee of objectivity. Impartiality is just a lack of critical self-awareness; it's failing to see how God has created us to take part in the mosaic of his people, to reflect the grandeur of God's kingdom. The result of such impartiality is subjectivism that refuses to be self-critical in reading the Bible. Everyone who reads the Bible operates with some kind of interest. The question for us, then, is whether we are willing to work toward reading the Bible within the church's rule of faith (dogmas)—the path in which the Spirit has guided and continues to guide the historic and global church in order to safeguard the reading of the Bible from the tyranny of "impartial" or self-proclaimed "objective" reading.

The Bible is the Word of God *and* becomes the Word of God to the truth-embodying community through the witness of the Holy Spirit when the church reads the Bible in the course of its own worship, preaching, liturgy, catechetics, prayer, care of souls, works of charity, and endurance of suffering. Christopher Hall, who teaches at Eastern University, concurs that learning to read the Bible in the context of church life will readily reveal the distorting effect of one's own cultural, historical, linguistic, philosophical and theological lens. Moreover, the best exegesis has taken place within the community of the church through the centuries. Hall maintains:

> The Bibles have been given to the church, are read, preached, heard and comprehended within the community of the church, and are safely interpreted only by those whose character is continually being formed by prayer, worship, meditation, self-examination, confession, and other means by which Christ's grace is communicated to his body. . . . This holistic, communal approach is surely a methodology that warrants a close investigation in our highly individualistic, specialized, segmented world.[8]

A question remains for the Asian American church as a truth-embodying community:

Can the Church, should the Church, read its Scriptures with any other guiding assumption than that in Jesus Christ, God has himself appeared in human history? We must not be too quick to answer. The question is not a purely theoretical one to be decided dispassionately. It is a question which reaches to the very heart of the Christian faith.[9]

3

HEALTHY LEADERS, HEALTHY HOUSEHOLDS 1

Challenges and Models

HELEN LEE

JOSEPH LEE HAD EVERY REASON TO FEEL OPTIMISTIC about the future of his ministry at Needham United Korean Presbyterian Church (NUKPC)*, an immigrant congregation in the suburbs of Boston. As an attendee since his teenage years, he had grown up in the church and knew many of its members in both the first-generation and English-speaking congregations. He had even decided to forgo his career in dentistry to pursue the ministry, and as the new full-time pastor for the English-speaking congregation, he was ready to apply concepts he'd learned from his time in seminary and from his own personal study of seeker-sensitive and Asian American ministries.

What was even better was that he had obtained the position on his terms, requesting autonomy for the English Ministry (EM) in three areas: finance, staffing and ministry direction. The leaders of the first generation congregation agreed to the terms, and for the first year the EM grew in size from 150 to 220 attendees. Lee made plans to begin a second, seeker-sensitive wor-

---

*Not the real name.

ship service in a more urban location, and he felt enthusiastic about where the ministry was headed.

But then the troubles began. First, Lee met with resistance from EM leaders about starting another service, particularly when the issue of money was involved. Although the conflict was ultimately resolved, Lee recalls, "I wanted this so much [that] I moved too fast without getting them on board." But then a more serious issue emerged between the EM and first-generation congregations, again revolving around the issue of money. "Our budget was increasing at such a rapid rate that we were catching up to the Korean congregation," says Lee. The leaders of the Korean congregation were uncomfortable with the budget the EM had requested and also began questioning how the EM was handling its finances, staffing and ministry plans. For six months the leaders of both congregations in the church tried to manage their differences. But ultimately no resolution emerged. Lee resigned from his position after two years, and many of his fellow EM leaders also left the church.

After his departure from NUKPC, Lee returned to the field of dentistry and now serves as a lay leader at Highrock Church, another Asian American church in the Boston area, which he feels is a much healthier congregation than what he experienced at NUKPC. NUKPC has since dramatically changed in composition and size. The Korean congregation began to have its own challenges and recently weathered a split, resulting in the loss of many of its first-generation members. In addition the church's EM has also since dissolved, an unfortunate end to a church ministry that used to serve a significant number of Asian American young people.

■ ■ ■

In his well-known book *Leadership Is an Art*, Max DePree writes, "The signs of outstanding leadership appear primarily among the followers. Are the followers reaching their potential? Are they learning? Serving? Do they achieve the required results? Do they change with grace? Manage conflict?"[1] In other words, in the context of the church, healthy congregations provide evidence of healthy leadership. Without effective leadership, churches often flounder, fail to achieve their full potential or in some cases disappear altogether.

"Leadership," says David Gibbons, senior pastor of NewSong Irvine, "is integral to the whole health of the church." The concept, while seemingly obvious, is at the same time difficult to achieve. And for Asian American pastoral leaders the challenge is increased by a host of cultural challenges that can often work in opposition to the goal of healthy leadership. In this chapter, we will examine some of these culture-influenced factors, and compare these traits to several key biblical models of leadership that can provide corrective aid for Asian American church leaders. In chapter four we will discuss a number of ways that leaders of healthy Asian American congregations build their churches, and the values they ascribe to in order to keep themselves and their congregations strong.

More than just community gatherings, healthy Asian American congregations are each representative households of God, each a part of the larger universal church bound together under the spiritual headship of Christ. The concepts discussed here are therefore not intended to merely increase the efficiency or relational connectedness of these churches, but aim for a loftier purpose: to help strengthen the family of God for the glory of God. Otherwise, if any part of the family struggles or suffers, the whole body of Christ is affected. Thus, in creating healthy and well-functioning Asian American churches, the stakes are high.

CULTURAL CHALLENGES TO HEALTHY ASIAN AMERICAN LEADERSHIP

In *Basic Christian Leadership* John Stott writes, "Our model of leadership is often shaped more by culture than by Christ. Yet many cultural models of leadership are incompatible with the servant imagery taught and exhibited by the Lord Jesus."[2] This may be nowhere truer than in the Asian American community, where culture continues to influence how leaders conduct themselves, whether the leaders realize it or not.

Four areas in particular can serve as stumbling blocks to the development of healthy Asian American churches and church leaders:

- Confucian-based perspectives
- false humility
- face-saving, shame-based approaches
- inability to resolve conflict

CONFUCIAN-BASED PERSPECTIVES

The ancient teachings of Confucius (551-479 B.C.) continue to have ramifications for today's Asian Americans, having played a significant role in the development of East Asian cultural thought for many centuries. In particular, Confucianism is defined by hierarchy and patriarchy—in the simplest terms, there is a distinct leadership structure defining who is above whom; that is, those who are younger serve those who are older, and women serve men. Myungseon Oh, who studied leadership within the Korean church, noted, "Due to such influences of Confucianism, Koreans tend to define all human relationships in terms of superior versus subordinate, the ruler versus the ruled, including gender and age. Such authoritarian persuasion permeates through the society."[3] It isn't a stretch to assume that similar attitudes exist elsewhere in East Asia, given the extent to which Confucianism has been absorbed by Chinese and Japanese cultures.

But, given the dramatic success of the Christian church in Korea since the 1800s, the intersection between Confucianism and church life is perhaps more pronounced than in other cultures, with the corresponding effect in the United States being felt just as strongly. Oh notes that Korean churches display a strong "authoritarian culture that is contradictory to Christian teaching" and, as a consequence, "the spiritual authority of pastors is seldom questioned."[4]

Even in the United States, first-generation Korean pastors have often espoused this hierarchy with their own ministries. Sociologist Karen J. Chai writes that "the ethnic church plays an important role in satisfying the needs for social status, prestige, power, and recognition within the immigrant community," and says that "it is no surprise that Korean immigrant churches have a more hierarchical leadership structure than American churches."[5] This in turn has affected those in later generations who have witnessed the leadership of the first generation and pursued Christian ministries themselves. In some cases, second-generation pastors have internalized similar attitudes, abusing their position or power, or wearing the mantle of leadership in such a way that expects subservience from those who are under their authority (particularly women).

Concurrently, Asian American congregants often place extraordinarily high expectations on their lead pastor and, if the pastor is male, elevate him to an unhealthy role of father figure. In addition, given the Asian tendency toward authoritarianism, members of Asian American congregations may not feel the freedom to disagree with pastoral leaders or even may be discouraged from doing so by the leader(s).

But clearly, a Confucian-based model of leadership runs counter to the teachings of Scripture. In his book *Escape from Church, Inc.*, E. Glenn Wagner writes:

> If we think of ourselves primarily as leaders or big shots, it is easy to start looking down on those who follow us. . . . When we consciously remember that we are shepherds, we remain humble. But when we start thinking of ourselves as leaders, humility tends to evaporate— sometimes, along with our ministry.[6]

FALSE HUMILITY

On the opposite end of the spectrum from excessive authoritarianism lies another cultural tendency of Asian Americans: displaying what appears to be humility in the guise of deference, deflection of compliments or resistance to stepping forward or speaking out on critical issues. As opposed to true humility, a more accurate way to term this type of behavior is *false humility*. For example, false humility occurs when a person knows deep within that they are competent and able to handle a proffered job but refuses the offer under the guise of humility, or when a person chooses not to make his or her opinions known to avoid potential conflict or embarrassment. Grace May, says:

> Most Asian Americans struggle with distinguishing between what is genuine, God-grown humility and what is false modesty, which is an aspect of our cultural heritage that we need to try to shake. It is not about technique or vocabulary but character. Only a Christ-like person can display genuine humility.

For female leaders, resisting false humility may prove even more challenging. May says:

> I've been doubly socialized to be humble, gracious, kind and forbearing. But there are times in ministry when being nice and kind has not served me or the body well. There are times when I felt I had to raise my voice to win respect. Humility does not mean being a doormat. The dilemma is that when I choose not to defer for fear of offending another person, I intrinsically feel that I am not being a good Asian woman or minister. It is as if I carry these pictures in my mind that to be "feminine" I must be deferential, and to be a minister I must be nice and not confrontational. So I confess that even when the Lord calls me to be assertive, sometimes I renege or hold back. I am so unaccustomed to speaking my mind in public or disagreeing with those that I respect, especially in Asian first-generation circles, that I ignore the Spirit's prompting and cave in to inertia and unhealthy patterns of relating. I am convinced that we would bless our churches and ourselves so much if we made a concerted effort to learn healthier ways of coping and dealing with our differences. Once redeemed, then, as the Asian American Church, we could offer our sense of etiquette and genuine humility to the larger household of God.

Ken Fong, senior pastor of Evergreen Baptist Church of Los Angeles, recently decided to take the radical step of lobbying for a raise, which he had never done before in more than twenty years of ministry at Evergreen. A friend had confronted him on this issue, saying that he was engaging in false humility by not believing that he deserved that raise. So he took the step of speaking with the church board, despite his trepidation at doing so. "I had been willing to sacrifice without the raise because it was my investment in helping the church get on its feet. But after it was on its feet, I did ask for more consideration in my salary," Fong says. "Especially in a Japanese context, which is the background of this church, to speak up for yourself is almost like committing suicide. But I learned that humility doesn't mean false humility. When you've done a good job, it's OK to say so."

Another way that false humility manifests itself in the Asian American church context is a tendency to avoid or shun leadership with an "I am not worthy" attitude. An oft-quoted Japanese expression—"The nail that sticks out gets hammered down"—aptly depicts the Asian nature not to unnecessarily stand out or put oneself forward. To do so is risky; it displays an individualism that often runs counter to the traditional collectivistic Asian mindset and is often perceived to be the wrong way to respond to invitations to lead. To accept such invitations would be a display of pride, not humility, or so the mentality goes.

As a result, Asian Americans who have been genuinely called to leadership may resist accepting the call, and Asian American churches find themselves struggling with staffing issues. Due to this tendency toward false humility, Asian American Christians are less inclined to volunteer for leadership positions, not wanting to communicate that they are more capable or gifted than others by putting forth their own name. Nancy Sugikawa, consulting pastor at Lighthouse Christian Church in Issaquah, Washington, and a former pastor at NewSong Church, reflects on the differences she saw working at a non-Asian church versus an Asian American church:

When I was at a primarily Caucasian church recruiting potential small group leaders, I found that people volunteered easily, even those who were new Christians or had never even been in a small group before. They were willing to try leading, even if it meant risking failure or rejection. In Asian churches people rarely volunteer for leadership positions. You have to personally approach and encourage them. Non-Asians seem to handle rejection better. If Asians are not accepted into leadership after volunteering, they would often feel a sense of shame or inadequacy, which might prevent them from ever volunteering again.

As Sugikawa notes, some Asian Americans find another reason to refuse overtures to participate: What if I were to lead but then fail? Again, the shame element prevents people from taking initiative to lead. This is an area in which Asian American church leaders will need to demonstrate creativity and sensitivity toward their congregations in order to generate enthusiasm for new leadership.

SAVING FACE AND AVOIDING SHAME

Asian Americans desperately want to avoid being shamed. What is shame? Christian psychologist Lewis Smedes defines shame, in contrast to grace, this way: "We feel guilty for what we *do*. We feel shame for what we *are*. . . . We may feel guilty because we lied to our mother. We may feel shame because we are not the persons our mother wanted us to be."[7]

Avoiding shame is woven deeply into the identity of Asians and, by extension, Asian Americans. In a study of Asian American college students, researchers Karen Huang and Christine Yeh discovered that "the process of ethnic identification is unique for Asian Americas in that shame . . . is a culturally powerful motivating force in defining oneself."[8] Avoiding shame is critical for Asian Americans, Huang and Yeh say, because "the social consequences often involve exclusion. For example, shaming can involve loss of support and confidence from one's family, community, or social network."[9]

Shaming occurs when a person "loses face." Huang and Yeh describe the process of losing face:

Asian culture teaches individuals to worry about how others will react so that they can maintain face. Face includes the positive image, interpretations or social attributes that one claims for oneself or perceives others to have accorded one. If one does not fulfill expectations of the self, then one loses face. . . . When one loses face, one feels tremendous shame.[10]

In the Asian American church context, leaders need to be sensitive to their members' need to save face and avoid shame. For example, it may be more difficult to find people who will share their testimonies and stories due to their unwillingness to let others see the conflicts or difficulties in their lives. In addition, leaders must take care not to unnecessarily shame their members as a motivational technique, which can occur in settings with overly authoritarian leaders.

But most important, Asian American church leaders must take the time to examine sources of healthy and unhealthy shame within themselves. Smedes says, "Many of us need to heal our unhealthy shame precisely so that we can recognize and do something about the healthy shame underneath it. . . . In the past I worried about complacent people who were blind to their own shortcomings. Now I worry about shamed people who are blind to their own strengths."[11]

In his book *Invitation to Lead* InterVarsity Christian Fellowship's National Asian American Ministry Coordinator, Paul Tokunaga, writes, "More than anything, those of us from shame-based cultures need to know and experience God's unconditional, unearnable love."[12] For those working in or entering into Asian American ministry, this is a critical step of personal development to help ensure the eventual growth of healthy congregations and members.

INABILITY TO RESOLVE CONFLICT

Asian American churches are not always adept at resolving conflicts. Coming from a cultural perspective that views conflict in a negative light, many Asian American church leaders have not had sufficient opportunities to practice healthy conflict resolution, either in their own personal relationships or in a congregational setting. But a prerequisite for developing healthy churches is accepting conflict as a natural byproduct of working with people, embracing it and dealing proactively with it when it occurs.

"In Asian Americans churches, often when there are disagreements, you are told to just deal with it. Sometimes, that may be true, but if something is bothering you, you have to be able to air it," says NewSong Church's Gibbons. "It's particularly difficult for Asian American leaders to do this with older or senior leaders. And when they do bring issues up, they do not do it in a healthy way. It usually will come out with a bite and with anger because it has been bottled up."

The American Korean immigrant church's tendency to split rather than work through differences is one example of what can happen when conflict is not resolved well (as seen in the story of NUKPC at the beginning of this chapter). For today's second-generation (and beyond) Asian American churches to avoid similar fates, they will need leaders who are proactive at managing and rooting out conflict, even if they have not had much experience doing so in a church context before. In chapter four, I will address this topic further and offer practical guidance on how to manage this critical area.

BIBLICAL MODELS OF HEALTHY LEADERSHIP

Despite the cultural challenges that Asian American leaders face, the Bible provides numerous examples of timeless leadership principles that apply regardless of the cultural setting. Models and principles of leadership are numerous, and I will not address the many concepts that exist in Christian management literature today. However, there are several biblical and theological principles manifested in the ministries of Moses and Jesus that are particularly relevant for current Asian American church leaders.

THE MODEL OF MOSES: RELUCTANT BUT PERSISTENT

In addition to his bicultural heritage as a Hebrew raised in an Egyptian culture, Moses displays several characteristics of particular relevance to Asian

American leaders: (1) although he is initially reluctant to lead, he chooses a life of obedience to God's call; (2) he displays significant humility; and (3) he demonstrates persistence and faithfulness in the enormous task of leading the Israelites to the Promised Land.

As previously mentioned, Asian American tendencies toward false humility and saving face moves them away from leadership. Moses can serve as a model for Asian American leaders in his example of being an initially reluctant leader. When God calls him to lead the Israelites out of Egypt, his first response is resistance. "Who am I that I should go to Pharaoh and bring the Israelites out of Egypt?" he queries (Ex 3:11). Asian Americans who sense a call to leadership but who simultaneously feel internal resistance preventing them from accepting such a call should find some reassurance that even Moses did not initially embrace leadership when called. But neither should they immediately dismiss the idea out of hand. Instead, they should be aware that their reluctance may be a product of their cultural upbringing or personality, and stay attuned to additional signs that God may be giving them to confirm that he desires they step into a leadership role.

Moses appears particularly concerned about his perceived inability to communicate verbally. "Pardon your servant, Lord. I have never been eloquent," he says. "I am slow of speech and tongue" (Ex 4:10). God dismisses this concern by telling Moses that he will help Moses, ultimately providing Moses' brother Aaron to handle speaking responsibilities. Asian American leaders can learn several things from this interaction. First, leaders do not always excel in all areas. And the pressure to be perfect that some Asian Americans feel intensely may cause them to focus on their perceived deficiencies rather than trusting and answering God's call to leadership.

A second lesson from Exodus 4 is that whatever deficiencies a leader may have—and every leader has shortcomings—God can more than compensate. As he says to Moses, "Who gave human beings their mouths? Who makes them deaf or mute? Who gives them sight or makes them blind? Is it not I, the LORD? Now go; I will help you speak and will teach you what to say" (Ex 4:11-12). When God calls a leader, he provides what the leader needs, whether it be wisdom, skills or partners. Asian American leaders who feel insecure or doubt their abilities can take comfort from Moses' example, resting assured that when God calls them to leadership, he will not abandon them in the midst of their weaknesses but will support them and demonstrate his power through them.

Ultimately, Moses obeys God; moreover, he eventually displays confidence in his speaking abilities. Starting at Exodus 8, Moses takes on more of the speaking role, to the point that by chapter 14 he addresses the Israelites directly, speaking compellingly with his exhortation, "Do not be afraid. Stand firm and you will see the deliverance the LORD will bring you today. The Egyptians you see today you will never see again" (Ex 14:13). God doesn't let Moses or today's church leaders linger in their weakness; he helps them manage those weaknesses, and ultimately, by God's grace, they can overcome those weaknesses, even turning them into strengths.

Two other notable traits that Moses displays through the course of his life are humility and faithfulness. Moses demonstrated humility soon after he had brought the Israelites out of captivity. His father-in-law, Jethro, witnessed how Moses was managing the people, and bluntly tells Moses, "What you are doing is not good" (Ex 18:17). Jethro subsequently suggests delegating most of Moses' judging responsibilities so that Moses can attend to the most important matters.

Many leaders struggle with receiving feedback, particularly negative feedback, because of pride. But Moses displays a necessary quality for healthy leaders: a teachable spirit. "As someone who's been in upper echelons of leadership, I'm not the best at taking criticism," says Soong-Chan Rah, senior pastor of Cambridge Community Fellowship Church. "But Moses' willingness to listen to the advice of his father-in-law shows humility and an acceptance that he cannot do the work alone. Receiving feedback is very important." It also provides a healthier perspective in contrast to the more authoritarian models of leadership that have characterized Asian Christian leaders in earlier generations. In the same way as Moses, Asian American Christian leaders need to be willing to acknowledge, with humility, that they both require and would benefit from the assistance and counsel of others. Toward the end of his ministry, the Bible notes that "Moses was a very humble man, more humble than anyone else on the face of the earth" (Num 12:3). His humble attitude was no doubt a key reason that he had the unique relationship with God he did, one in which "the LORD would speak to Moses face to face, as one speaks to a friend" (Ex 33:11).

As for Moses' faithfulness, his leadership of the Israelites spanned forty years, which in and of itself is an accomplishment. But what is even more commendable is that he was faithful in his ministry even when the very people he was trying to lead turned against him or failed him, which they did numerous times. His compassion is so strong for the Israelites that when God is ready to abandon them, Moses advocates on their behalf. In Numbers 14 the Israelites are close to entering the Promised Land. But they focus more on the short-term difficulties and begin to rebel. "All the Israelites grumbled against Moses and Aaron, and the whole assembly said to them, 'If only we died in the Egypt! . . . We should choose a leader and go back to Egypt'" (Num 14:2, 4).

Church leaders will often experience hardships that arise from issues within their own flock. Sometimes their own people will doubt them, publicly or privately; some church members will openly complain or harbor negative feelings toward their leaders. Moses could have chosen many courses of action to handle the rebellious outbreak. But he demonstrates his humility once again, falling "facedown in front of the whole Israelite assembly" (Num 14:5), and asking for their trust and support. Even God is tired of the Israelites' lack of faith and again wants to destroy them, but Moses steps in to ask forgiveness on behalf of his people. It's a remarkable response, given what he has been through with the Israelites, who were ready to stone him for their perceived hardship.

For today's Asian American church leaders, who will no doubt experience their own hardship within their congregations, Moses provides an example of steadfast, faithful perseverance even in the midst of life-threatening resistance. Although there are times when walking away from a ministry is appropriate and necessary, too often in today's culture of instant gratification leaders are not inclined to persevere in the midst of difficult situations, particularly when they feel attacked. But Moses provides a picture of what a leader with a long-term perspective and persistence can accomplish. In the end his stature in Judeo-Christian history is well-deserved, in large part due to his extraordinary and faithful leadership.

THE MODEL OF JESUS: SERVANT, PROPHET, VISIONARY

If Moses' humility was perhaps initially derived from a sense of insecurity, Jesus came from a completely different place, aware as he was of his identity and position as the Son of God and yet a human being. Yet Jesus too demonstrated a radical humility. And through his servant attitude, his ability to speak hard truths with a prophetic, forward-looking voice, and his example in envisioning and communicating the future kingdom of God, he can certainly serve as a model for Asian American leaders.

Although the concept of Jesus as a servant leader is familiar for many of today's Christians, during the time of Jesus' ministry even his closest disciples had difficulty grasping the idea. Despite having spent three years alongside Jesus, during the Last Supper the disciples were still arguing over which of them was the greatest. Discouraging though this might have been for Jesus, through an unforgettable act he models how he wants his disciples to treat others: he gets up and begins to wash his disciples' feet. Before Jesus starts, John writes that "Jesus knew that the Father had put all things under his power, and that he had come from God and was returning to God" (Jn 13:3). Yet despite this knowledge of his exalted position in the universe, Jesus consciously chooses to display an attitude befitting someone completely opposite: someone who would be considered the least, not the greatest, the servant rather than the one to be served.

Peter's visceral reaction to Jesus' attempt to wash his feet is immediate. He instantly recognizes that something is amiss, and he cannot accept it. "No, you shall never wash my feet," he declares (Jn 13:8). Knowing what he does of Jesus' status as the Messiah, the Son of God, Peter finds it inconceivable to let Jesus anywhere near his dirty feet. And yet Jesus persists, letting Peter know that this is the type of kingdom he stands for. "Do you understand what I have done for you?" he asks. "Now that I, your Lord and Teacher, have washed your feet, you also should wash one another's feet. I have set you an example that you should do as I have done for you" (Jn 13:14-15).

Reflecting on lessons he has learned about Christian leadership while living and working at the L'Arche communities for mentally handicapped people in Toronto, Henri Nouwen writes about Jesus' example of servanthood in his classic book, *In the Name of Jesus*. Nouwen says that the most important quality of Christian leadership is

> not leadership of power and control, but a leadership of powerlessness and humility in which the suffering servant of God, Jesus Christ, is made manifest. . . . I am speaking of a leadership in which power is constantly abandoned in favor of love. It is true spiritual leadership. Powerlessness and humility in the spiritual life do not refer to people who have no spine and who let everyone else make decisions for them. They refer to people who are so deeply in love with Jesus that they are ready to follow him wherever he guides them, always trusting that, with him, they will find life and find it abundantly.[13]

Although it may be easy for today's Asian American Christian leaders to agree with Nouwen's perspective in theory, the reality is that these leaders may experience temptations and struggles with wanting to achieve and succeed just as much in the ministry field as they have been encouraged to do all their lives. Along with cultural models that display more of an authoritarian example of leadership, these temptations can trap people into modes of thinking and acting as leaders that result in a focus on self-achievement and progress rather than on Christ's example of humble servitude.

Rah notes that particularly for younger Asian Americans, there is reason to reexamine and refocus on this aspect of Jesus' leadership style. "The idea of servant leadership is critical for Asian American church leaders," he says.

Second-generation Asian Americans are often thrown into leadership early by virtue of need, and one of the major dangers of that process, and of being a senior pastor at age twenty-seven or twenty-eight, is that you think you know everything. You think you can make unilateral decisions without processing them through. But Jesus' humility is the counteragent to that attitude. We are often getting too much, too soon—too much authority, and too much responsibility. We need to balance that with humility.

In addition to Jesus' lifestyle of servanthood and humility, he also demonstrated a principle of leadership that is often difficult for Asian Americans: the ability to speak truthfully and prophetically. When the circumstances required a direct and blunt response, Jesus was willing to make the necessary point. Perhaps one of the most striking examples of this principle comes in John 2, when Jesus clears the temple of merchants who are selling animals intended for sacrifices. When Jesus sees this, his response is unequivocal and dramatic: "He made a whip out of cords, and drove all from the temple courts, both sheep and cattle; he scattered the coins of the money changers and overturned their tables. To those who sold doves he said, 'Get these out of here! Stop turning my Father's house into a market!'" (Jn 2:15-16).

An Asian American in Jesus' shoes at that moment may have taken another route to deal with the situation. Perhaps he or she would have just sidestepped the incident, because the thought of creating such a public outcry would be too unthinkable. Or perhaps another option would have been to try to find a less overt way to confront the merchants in order not to be perceived as a rabble-rouser or troublemaker. But Jesus knew that he had to make a statement because these merchants were using space intended for worship for their own gain. Jesus' willingness to embrace difficult situations and cause the necessary conflicts is a challenge for Asian American leaders to emulate, especially in the church context where a propensity for demonstrating "unity in Christ" often hinders necessary truth-telling. While Jesus' divinity allowed him to know how to perfectly address each conflict, human beings are not similarly blessed, which can result in doubt or uncertainty in how to handle such situations. (One potential danger for those leaders who are trying to develop a more prophetic voice is that they need to be well connected with God and with his Word in order to ensure that their proclamations are coming from a divine and not merely human source.) But on the balance, Asian Americans tend to avoid or resist opportunities to engage in direct truth-telling when the situation calls for it.

Ken Fong of Evergreen Baptist Church-LA faced a situation in which one of his part-time staff had an affair. She confessed the sin to her husband and to Fong, and he felt pressure to publicly inform the congregation that she was taking a leave of absence and leave it at that. But he decided instead to bring the truth to light, with the woman and her family's permission and support.

> I told the whole congregation what had happened, that this woman had been unfaithful to her husband, that she had resigned from our staff and that we need to pray for her. Some people came to me and said that I had shared too much information. That's a very Asian response. But in the twenty-first century, people are looking to church leaders who are willing to talk about the things that need to be talked about. Sometimes, boldness means you have to get out of the Asian culture. I think we miss all kinds of redemptive moments because we keep playing the culture card.

This tendency to avoid prophetic truth-telling also affects the way that Asian American churches handle their approach in ministering to the world outside their doors. Rah says, "Jesus was not afraid to address the social ills, and to confront the existing power structures. This is something that is missing on a corporate level among Asian American Christians." Although Asian American churches are doing more on an individual level to confront societal problems such as racism, poverty and injustice, a communal voice against such issues has not yet emerged. NewSong Church's Gibbons says, "What's missing in the Asian American church is the prophetic voice. That includes advocacy for the poor, the oppressed and the outcasts of society.

Leaders have to see God's heart for the misfit, for the weak. We need more Malcolm Xs, at least in terms of the fire and the passion. We need more courageous leaders."

Last, Jesus focused on the future and excelled in communicating this future to those living in his present time. In his teachings Jesus frequently makes reference to the kingdom of God, and he paints many pictures for his disciples of what that unseen future kingdom would be like. Jesus is not content to live in the present age and overthrow earthly establishments and rulers for the sake of a temporary reign; he is interested in an eternal victory, and repeatedly provides his followers with mental images and words to grasp the larger drama they were participating in, such as in this passage from Matthew:

> Truly I tell you, at the renewal of all things, when the Son of Man sits on his glorious throne, you who have followed me will also sit on twelve thrones, judging the twelve tribes of Israel. And everyone who has left houses or brothers or sisters or father or mother or wife or children or fields for my sake will receive a hundred times as much and will inherit eternal life. But many who are first will be last, and many who are last will be first. (Mt 19:28-29)

Similarly, Asian American church leaders must also be visionary leaders. One of their key responsibilities is to ascertain the vision that God is giving them regarding their churches and to communicate that vision to their staff and congregations. This is often more difficult than it sounds due to human (and Asian American) nature, which prefers to avoid change (see chap. 5). But strong Asian American church leaders are not satisfied with status quo. They press on toward the goal given to them by God—even if others do not always understand what they are doing.

"People need lots and lots of help getting the vision and staying excited about it," says Evergreen Baptist Church-LA's Fong.

> Whoever is going to be the pastor of an Asian American congregation, and who desires to have their church make a difference and have in-

fluence for Christ's sake, has to say, "This is where we start but we will not stay this way due to the Holy Spirit. We will die to ourselves and break down the dividing walls of hostility that surround us." It may take our lifetimes, but the longer we are here on earth, the more we should be a preview, bit by bit, of the coming attractions.

Although there are many challenges to healthy Asian American church leadership, biblical models such as those provided by Moses and Jesus can help leaders to overcome those challenges and build healthy households of God in their ministries. In chapter four we will examine one of the most critical aspects of creating these households: building and maintaining healthy leadership teams.

4

HEALTHY LEADERS, HEALTHY HOUSEHOLDS 2

Practices and Values

HELEN LEE

JOHN CHANG, PASTOR OF AN ASIAN AMERICAN CHURCH in suburban Washington, D.C., hung up the phone and massaged his aching temples. He had just gotten off the phone with Kevin, a member of his elder board who had given him an earful of information he did not want to hear. Kevin had become embroiled in a conflict with Jenny, another elder, to the point that they were barely on speaking terms, making it difficult to have effective board meetings of late. When Kevin and Jenny joined the board two years earlier, they were casual friends but had not worked together in a close context. Being a part of the board had exposed their differing personality and work styles, and over time those differences had resulted in conflicts of growing magnitude. Pastor Chang felt that it was important not to interfere because he didn't want to be perceived as taking sides. He also wanted Kevin and Jenny to work out their differences directly with one another, as he had hinted to both on several occasions. He was surprised to discover that Kevin wanted to resign from the board, and furthermore that Kevin was now equally frustrated with Pastor Chang for what he described "a complete lack of action and direction" in this matter. The pastor was not sure what he should do at this point and also wondered what he could have done, if anything, to intervene in a way that would have prevented the conflict in the first place. The only thing he did know was that dealing with a situation like this was stressful and draining. He wished that he could just say a prayer and see the whole mess disappear.

■ ■ ■

Leadership guru Peter Drucker once said, "Whenever you see a successful business, someone once made a courageous decision." The same principle applies in the church context as well. The path to guiding and growing a healthy congregation lies in myriad decisions that have to be made along the way, many of which have to do with creating quality relationships among pastoral and lay leaders. In this chapter, we will see how a number of current church leaders built and grew their leadership teams. The chapter will also cover several key values these leaders abide by in their quest to build their congregations into healthy households of God.

BUILDING HEALTHY LEADERSHIP TEAMS

As Jesus himself demonstrated, ministry is not meant to be accomplished by lone rangers. His example to call twelve, to focus on three and to send his disciples out to minister by pairs indicate his desire to promote teamwork when it came to accomplishing his mission on earth. Even now, thousands of years later, the same principle remains. "Ministry is a communal and mutual experience," writes Henri Nouwen in *In the Name of Jesus*. "Indeed, whenever we minister together, it is easier for people to recognize that we do not come in our own name, but in the name of the Lord Jesus who sent us."[1]

Building and maintaining strong leadership teams is a challenging activity. It requires being able to accurately assess your own personality and gifts, and those of your teammates, a process that often initially occurs with limited information. Then it requires a steadfast and proactive commitment to good communication and conflict resolution in order to develop strong relationships that can weather the inevitable challenges. Some might think a solo ministry opportunity is more attractive because of the opportunity to have more ownership and authority as a leader, but even in that context a solo pastor will have to work with a lay leadership team or board. Thus good teamwork is necessary in any ministry setting, and the payoff can be significant. When leaders work together well, the synergy that results can be the mysterious X-factor that separates healthy and effective congregations from unhealthy and unproductive ones.

Strong leadership teams can serve a unique function that is particularly relevant for Asian Americans, according to pastor Dihan Lee of Open Door Presbyterian Church in Herndon, Virginia:

> For Asian American leaders, a team context is very valuable because I think many of us come from a home context where there is not much vulnerability or opportunity to have your gifts appreciated and valued—instead, there's an emphasis on academic achievement and obedience. So if you minister by yourself, you have a blind spot for the areas you need to improve, and you need affirmation for other areas. In a team context, you can really explore gifting and have accountability from other people. Good team ministry is not just about having one person handle the youth group and another handle the junior high. A strong team is one with a sense of community and family, which is absolutely critical for the Asian American context. How you do life within that team will be a reflection of how it is done within the church.

One challenge for Asian American church leaders, however, is that either they or those with whom they are working (lay leaders or fellow staff) might not have had sufficient experience in high-quality teams. For many individuals the point at which they develop their first and most basic teamwork-related skills is in the family, but many Asian American families do not operate with teamwork-like principles. Instead of practicing open conflict resolution, conflict is often avoided, and the Confucian influence results in parents asserting their authority without allowing much opportunity for teamwork and partnership. "Younger generations want to have some sense of team, but they do not have the tools to live that out," says Soong-Chan Rah, senior pastor of Cambridge Community Fellowship Church (Cambridge, Mass.). "Or in some cases, the immigrant-family experience meant an absence of parenting influence, and a loss of a sense of family dynamics. This can result in people who desire the community experience without a real understanding of what it means to get there."

Thus the quality of the relationships in the leadership team can significantly affect the health of an Asian American congregation. When a leadership team exhibits a strong sense of family and community, it becomes a model for the whole church. A leadership team and its congregation will benefit from community characterized by honesty, loving care, good communication and camaraderie, and these only come from a significant and intentional investment of time and energy from the team members.

How does a church build and maintain a high-quality, healthy leadership team? The congregations represented in this book recommend a number of ways to do so:

- choose and use team members well
- build trust among leaders
- pursue conflict resolution vigorously
- cultivate the vision

CHOOSE AND USE TEAM MEMBERS WELL

For the past few years *Christianity Today* magazine and the Best Christian Workplaces Institute have cosponsored an annual survey called "The Best Christian Places to Work." One of the consistent findings from that survey, year in and year out, is that great places to work devote significant time and energy in finding the right people to work in their organizations. They recognize that the investment of resources to gather the right employees will result in greater productivity among the staff. The same principle applies in the church context: it takes time and effort to find the right people to work together on a leadership team, whether they will be paid staff or volunteer lay leaders. And then it takes even more time and effort to help those leaders work to the best of their ability.

When it comes to finding volunteer or lay leaders, Asian American churches often face a number of problems. On one hand, for young churches or church plants there is a significant temptation to appoint leaders who may not be ready or qualified for a leadership position, rather than waiting until the right leaders can be found. But rushing people into leadership due to perceived ministry needs can ultimately backfire on a church and produce conflicts that cause more trouble than if the church had waited for the right people.

On the other hand, Asian Americans tend to resist volunteering or promoting themselves as leaders due to their cultural upbringing. "If you stand up and say, 'I want to be a leader,' people question your motivation," says Evergreen Baptist Church-LA's executive pastor Jonathan Wu. "Is it your pride or ego, people wonder? And so you end up with a more passive congregation, with people who do not feel they are leaders. We have many gifted people at our church, but they do not feel their skills and competencies are what the church needs."

As a result today's healthy Asian American churches are intentionally recasting their language with lay leaders and encouraging them to recruit not only leaders but servants. "Asian Americans will often not see themselves as leaders, even if they are. So I try not to get stuck in saying that everybody has to be a leader," says Wayne Ogimachi, senior pastor of Lighthouse Christian Church in Issaquah, Washington. "But everybody is called to *ministry*. While we want to give attention to leadership development, we also need to legitimize that everybody has a calling from God to ministry."

In addition to hiring and recruiting the right people for paid and volunteer leadership and staff positions, healthy congregations place leaders in roles that best fit their particular skills and interests. In his business bestseller *Good to Great,* author Jim Collins uses the analogy of a bus to describe the process of putting together the right team of people in a corporate setting. He believes that a company not only needs to get the right people on the bus, but it also needs to discern with people that they are each sitting in the right seat. Neither task is simple nor straightforward, and given that people grow and change over time, getting them into the right seat is a process that must constantly be evaluated and tweaked when necessary.

Concurrent with the need to get people into the right seats is the corollary that even if people are in the right place, they still may need assistance and training to be able to be effective. Churches with healthy leadership teams are constantly evaluating how each person is doing, whether staff members are working in a manner befitting their gifts, and how to help people improve in their respective roles. "Leaders have to be developed," says senior pastor David Gibbons of NewSong Church (Irvine, Calif.). "It has to be intentional, and there has to be a clear process to train them."

Even for churches who do not have the resources of a larger congregation, training and development of volunteers is still critical. But Greg Yee, director of leadership and congregational development for the Pacific Southwest Conference of the Evangelical Covenant Church, says, "Lay leadership training only works well when the pastor believes in it. It takes blood, sweat and tears. All pastors say it is important, but not all pastors will go the distance required to make it work. A pastor has to invest in it, has to make it a priority, for it to work."[2]

BUILD TRUST AMONG LEADERS

Once the right leaders are chosen, the next significant task is for these leaders to learn to trust one another. Leaders of healthy congregations know that one of the most important things they can do with one another is to spend time together developing their personal and working relationships. This investment usually results in greater team camaraderie, which helps communication to flow more easily. But it also allows team members to better understand one another's perspectives, passions and gifts, which in turn helps build the foundation for trust to develop within a leadership team. The following story illustrates the lengths to which a pastoral team went in order to build a strong bond among the leaders of Korean-speaking and English-speaking congregations within the same church.

They Must Bowl!

By Dihan Lee, Open Door Presbyterian Church

Late one snowy evening in a remote town in Northern Virginia, five pastors from Open Door Presbyterian Church—one first-generation, two 1.5-generation and two second-generation pastors—are packed into one car, driving around looking for a bowling alley that still might be open. The road conditions are hazardous, but the car that carries the pastors continues to wind its way up and down the treacherous country roads. The pastors are committed to their declared fellowship activity. They must bowl; nothing will deter them.

This silly but determined endeavor to bowl illustrates how committed these pastors are to team building. They have just spent three days together at their third annual pastoral-staff retreat, during which their main aim was to enjoy one another and to strengthen their friendship and partnership in ministry. They bowled and laughed, shared about their lives, and dreamed together about what their church could be. It was less a retreat and more, as one second-generation pastor called it, a "family getaway."

To come to such a place of friendship and mutual trust, this pastoral staff team has had to work on its relationship building for many years. Partly, this intentional effort resulted from a painful past experience, namely, a clash between the pastoral staff members of the two congregations, causing a pastor and some of the lay leaders of the second-generation congregation to leave the church. Since then, the staff team has made team building a very high priority. In addition to their weekly staff meetings, they gather regularly for lunch. After discovering they all enjoy fishing, the staff team has gone on a number of day-long fishing trips to the Maryland shorelines, often failing to catch anything but always returning home with a deeper sense of belonging.

The Open Door pastoral team continues to encounter various intergenerational and intercultural conflicts that emerge as the Korean-speaking and the English-speaking congregations wrestle with what it means to be interdependent and to forge a new partnership. [See chap. 7 for more details on developing intergenerational partnership.] However, the staff team has learned to stand together in working through challenging situations and thorny issues. In many ways, the level of trust and the type of relationship built within the staff team are enabling the pastors to work through matters as family and are modeling Christ to their own respective congregations. "As the staff goes, so goes the church," observed a young member of this pastoral staff team.

So driving around looking for a bowling alley in the middle of a snowstorm may not have been a silly, wasteful activity after all.

Building trust through teamwork is not necessarily a smooth or quick process. Sometimes, the time it takes to forge a strong team is measured not in weeks or months but years. Grace May, former pastor of the Chinese Christian Church of New England, says that building a leadership team was one of her biggest challenges, in part because of how time intensive getting to know her lay leaders was. She says:

On the one hand, it is difficult to get to know people well enough to know how much they can bear, or what they find burdensome and draining versus what they want to embrace as a challenge. On the other hand, I may have spent hours in successive weeks with one leader. Then just as I begin to coalesce with that person, a new election or crisis crops up. But is the time worth it? Yes! In fact, one of the advantages that I find in serving in an Asian context is that I can invest so much time and energy in relationships. And it is in those extended amounts of time together—praying, sharing, eating and playing—that we are able to go deep.

The fruit that emerges from a foundation of trust among team members can be quite profound. Current research on organizational behavior consistently identifies trust as a key component to a company's success, and the same is often true in the church context. Without trust among leaders, as well as between leaders and those whom they are leading, progress will be much slower and fraught with conflicts than in healthy congregations where trust is cultivated and maintained. For example, Ken Fong, senior pastor of Evergreen Baptist Church-LA, notes that

> the number one pitfall for Asian American churches is micromanaging the staff. If you are a small church and the only staff member is the pastor with a volunteer staff of leaders, the danger is that your board meetings are still about the nuts and bolts of running the ministry rather than making sure the policies are already in place to do the right ministry. We don't want to have people who have to keep running back to the board whenever they have a question.

In other words, trust enables a church's top leaders to release volunteers to do the ministry. Thus the church's progress toward its mission doesn't have to get bogged down.

In addition, leadership teams characterized by trust tend to be willing to try out new ideas more readily, and they more easily embrace and overcome failure when it occurs. In *Leading the Team-Based Church,* author George Cladis writes, "Ministry teams that risk, fail, learn and grow are more likely to . . . find ways to communicate the Gospel than are teams that are fixed in rigid patterns. The postmodern characteristic of risk and discover fits well the biblical mandate to venture out into new lands with the Gospel."[3] In churches where there is healthy trust, people have more autonomy to make decisions and more leeway to attempt new programs or projects, and they don't feel restrained by needing approval for every decision. Trust and alignment toward a common mission allow for these types of healthy interactions to occur.

Investing in lay leaders who ultimately carry the burden of serving the church's day-to-day needs is a key part of building trust within the church. "I spend a lot of time making sure we have a healthy leadership team," says Steve Wong, lead pastor of Grace Community Covenant Church in Los Altos, California. Grace Community has both an elected elder board as well as a larger group of lay leaders called their ministry team. "I invest a lot in the ministry team heads, because if they are not shepherded well, issues can result," says Wong.

At Lighthouse Christian Church, senior pastor Wayne Ogimachi holds a monthly gathering for "any Christ follower committed to attending, serving and financially supporting Lighthouse." During these "ministry community meetings," Ogimachi covers any number of topics, from church business to the mission and vision of the church to handling any problems or issues that arise. He explains:

> Many churches have membership meetings that are occasional and only for church business. But sometimes we're so busy doing ministry that we don't get to hang out enough and share, or receive teaching on what the vision of the church is. In terms of our church's health it has been an important gathering to keep us focused, aligned, and encouraged. I think it's actually been one of the best things we've done.

By gathering his key leaders on a regular basis and ensuring they are well-informed and continually reminded of the mission of Lighthouse, Ogimachi is helping to make sure that the level of trust among his leaders is high.

PURSUE CONFLICT RESOLUTION VIGOROUSLY

Despite a congregation's best efforts to build strong, trusting relationships among its pastoral and lay leaders, conflicts can still occur. But given Asian influences, many Asian American churches find themselves paralyzed when the inevitable conflicts arise. Many church leaders interviewed for this book identified the inability to deal with conflict as the main cause behind unhealthy Asian American churches. In contrast, healthy congregations take a proactive approach and attitude toward conflict: they take preemptive measures against it, and when it emerges, they handle it quickly instead of allowing it to fester and be destructive within the church.

Lighthouse's Ogimachi says, "We just keep talking about conflict as a way to normalize it. That way, when it occurs in our church, it doesn't mean that it has to blow up our relationships and our congregation." Ogimachi brings the topic up frequently in his sermons: "Every year we do some kind of relationship series in the spring, such as a marriage series, and in the process we talk about how to have healthy relationships, which includes confrontation, forgiveness, the sharing of your feelings, listening skills, humility, commitment and so forth. That helps to address many congregational health issues."

In 1997 the leaders of Evergreen Baptist Church-LA came to a momentous and critical decision regarding the future of the church, deciding to "hive" the church into two congregations as a way to help increase the ministry of the church overall (see chap. 7, "Openness to Change"). The event could have become so full of conflict that neither congregation would have been able to move forward. However, the church and its leaders handled the situation proactively instead of trying to minimize and downplay the effects of the decision. Executive pastor Jonathan Wu recalls:

> When people were feeling the pain of the imminent hive, the pastoral staff developed a curriculum to help guide the congregation through the process. We addressed how to be at peace with one another, how to not just run away from the pain but to experience God's blessing through it. And though it did not resolve all the conflicts, it helped to provide a positive response to them.

NewSong Church's David Gibbons strongly believes that healthy conflict resolution must be vigorously pursued. "Conflict resolution is the thing that can kill a church emotionally and spiritually," he cautions. In the following interview, Gibbons offers the following thoughts about how his church makes conflict resolution a priority:

Q: Why is conflict resolution so difficult in Asian American churches?

A: In Asian American churches, people have a tendency not to air their grievances. But eventually, if you don't share your concerns, dissonance occurs. Then a second problem comes when people do not bring up their issues in a healthy manner. What needs to be done is to speak the truth in love; they speak truth but not in love. The third challenge is to say "I'm sorry" if you're wrong, as well as to forgive freely. If there's a sense of disagreement in an Asian American context, there's a tendency to be aloof. If there's a problem, you stay apart. You have to have intentionality about coming together.

Q: What are the key things you try to do at NewSong to have healthy conflict resolution?

A: First of all, we talk about it through our teaching. We use several mantras regularly, such as a "theology of discomfort." We build in the expectation that people will experience conflict, that it is normative here in healthy relationships. We also call it the last 10 percent. The last 10 percent is when you come to a point in a relationship where you are bothered by something in a person or about the person. You have a choice to deal with it or let it go and move toward aloneness. So we have a culture where conflict resolution is not abnormal but normal. We emphasize making the extra effort to go deeper with others. We also explain to people our family backgrounds and the dysfunctions that are there. For example, in the Asian context, people tend to hint at the issue and orbit it like the sun whereas typical Americans are known to go right at it. Last, we try to demonstrate healthy conflict resolution through our own modeling as leaders. If people on the staff are at odds with one another, we show the church how we deal with it. We talk about this issue in our membership class because one of our values is conflict resolution. We mention clearly how to go through the Matthew 18 process. If someone offends you, it's your job to go to that person, and we talk about how that looks and how you do that. This way you build trust with people, you stop gossip, and you move toward oneness.

Another significant thing we try to do is provide healthy conflict resolution through pastoral counseling or small group leadership training. We usually have seminars or an orientation on how to work through conflict. Pastoral counseling is a big piece of that. How you resolve conflict is usually the test of a deep community. The benefit from doing it well is deeper maturity and intimacy.

Q: What specifically should pastoral leaders do when they discover conflict occurring in their churches?

A: When we pastors find conflict going on, part of our leadership role is to make sure it's addressed, or help if those involved need it. A leader needs to model good conflict resolution when trying to deal with people in conflict. I often share personal examples with the church, such as how I resolved particular conflicts with my wife or with a fellow member of my staff. Conflict is a good sign that people are getting closer. So it's important to also highlight the positive contribution of conflict.

A good rule of thumb that I tell people is to use the twenty-four-hour principle. If you can't shake a bad feeling within twenty-four hours, you have to go talk to the person. Another rule of thumb is, if you can't look a person in the eye, or if you don't want to touch the person, those are some practical ways you know you are probably not in healthy relationship with him or her.

In the church, health has to start with leadership. If leadership is unhealthy, the church is unhealthy. That's why we demand that our staff really work through this. You don't know how many times we've had hash-out sessions. It's said there are four stages of team building: forming, storming, norming, performing. For us to get to that place where we'll really groove, we have to work hard on resolving conflict as a management and pastoral team.

In Asian culture, conflict is evidence that someone has done something wrong in the context of a relationship. But in American culture, conflict is a normal byproduct of human relationships. Today's healthy Asian American churches attempt to claim the good from both cultures: encouraging people to take responsibility when they have made errors that affect their fellow colleagues or believers in the church, but also challenging them to embrace and work through conflict when it occurs. In *The Fifth Discipline,* business strategist Peter Senge writes, "Conflict is a reliable indicator of a team that is continually learning. . . . In great teams, conflict becomes productive."[4] Leaders in healthy Asian American churches reflect this philosophy and have found ways to turn conflicts into opportunities for growth and progress in their congregations.[5]

CULTIVATE AND CAST THE VISION

One key way that leaders help reduce conflicts within a church is to cultivate and share a common commitment to the vision of the church, then to pass that vision onto the members of the congregation. But as evidenced by the amount of literature that has been written on the topic, this is no easy task. Still, healthy Asian American leaders have a significant advantage over secular businesses in the quest to find a vision for their congregations: as they seek God's path for their church, they often find that the vision comes to them. "Vision is the product of God working in us," says Terry Fullam, an Episcopal priest. "He creates the vision, and we receive it; it becomes a rallying point, a goal toward which we move as his people. Without it, as the Scripture says, 'the people perish.'"[6]

Setting a vision is much more than creating strategic plans or goals for the church's future; it involves engaging in a spiritual dynamic with God to determine his mind and heart for the congregation. Nor is developing an effective vision a purely solitary endeavor. Although many of the leaders interviewed for this book feel that vision-setting and casting largely occurs with their initiative and leading, none would claim that they have had the sole hand in developing their church's vision. And it is precisely the communal aspect of developing a vision that makes it all the more difficult—yet all the more powerful—when the process comes to fruition. Senge writes:

> Visions that are truly shared take time to emerge. They grow as a byproduct of interactions of individual visions. Experience suggests that visions that are genuinely shared require ongoing conversation where individuals not only feel free to express their dreams, but learn how to listen to each other's dreams. Out of this listening, new insights into what is possible gradually emerge.[7]

In healthy Asian American churches there is a strong sense that the vision of the church is not just embraced by the senior pastor or a handful of top leaders, but that it is shared more broadly within the congregation because it has been invited into the process of owning the vision's creation.

The challenge for Asian American church leaders is to know how and when to push for greater consensus when fellow congregants aren't on the same page, and how much agreement is enough. Healthy churches have leaders who are sensitive to their congregations; they listen to their fellow leaders and members as well as to God's voice to know best how to proceed. Due to the Asian cultural leaning to all be of the same mind in decision making, the felt need for consensus is particularly strong in the Asian American church. And indeed, churches with broad support and commitment to a shared vision will be more effective in the long run. But building consensus does not necessarily mean that every single person in the church will agree with the leaders or even that all leaders will agree. As Fullam notes, "The unity need only be as broad as the group having the authority. . . . Our goal is not to maintain unity. Our goal is to move under the headship of Christ. Unity is simply the gift he gives us when we find his mind."[8] Each congregation will have to determine its own "consensus point," whether that means a majority of senior leaders or a majority of its membership. But in any case, consensus in and of itself is not the ultimate goal; determining God's will for the church is the key focal point.

The process of "finding God's mind" when it comes to the vision of the church is far from a one-time event or simple procedure. In most cases it is an ongoing process, one that requires constant tweaking and refining, requiring hard work on the part of the leadership to do well, particularly when leaders attempt to invite the rest of the congregation into the discussion. When NewSong Church's Gibbons felt strongly that God had given him a new vision and direction for the church, one which was committed to a ministry of "justice, advocacy and compassion" (JAC), he and his leaders planned multiple avenues of communication with the broader church to slowly build the vision throughout the congregation:

> We knew it would be hard for our suburban, upper-middle-class church to embrace. So instead of just saying "this is what we're going to do," we worked to build consensus. I wanted everyone to hear God's heart on this, so we did a ten-week sermon series on this topic. We took "Vision Trips" to see what God was doing in other geographical locations in this ministry. We did prayer walks. We read books, interviewed other leaders in this area. I felt personally I had to model it, and I gave 10 percent of my time toward it. Eventually, people started to buy into it, and we helped them find opportunities to serve in this ministry. So my job is to try to figure out where God's hand is moving, and then if our church isn't quite there yet, I try to build consensus through leadership. Building consensus is not saying "what's everyone's opinion?" It's asking, "What does God want us to do, and what do people in our church feel that God is saying?"

No matter how a leader chooses to invite others into sharing the vision, however, the responsibility for cultivating and casting it largely sits on the shoulder of the church's senior pastor. And it is a responsibility that cannot be taken lightly. As Fullam notes, "For a lot of clergy, their vision is essentially limited to the expectations of the people around them. No wonder they get bogged down. Our vision must not be confined to our circumstances, or it will be forever small. It must instead be a vision engendered by the Scripture and supported by the Spirit."[9]

VALUES TO PURSUE AS YOU SERVE

No two leaders are exactly alike. Each has been shaped by experiences and influences that guide how he or she leads, and the many examples provided by those leaders interviewed in this book are a testimony to that reality. Even if the specific ways in which the values manifest themselves may look different from person to person, many of these individuals cited similar values they strive to live by as leaders. Although there are numerous values that could be listed, four were particularly notable in today's leaders of healthy Asian American congregations:

- pursuing a balanced life
- demonstrating vulnerability
- valuing team ministry
- recognizing God's leadership

PURSUING A BALANCED LIFE

For Asian American pastors who have seen first-generation Asian pastors performing their duties at a great level of personal cost and sacrifice, it may be difficult to let go of that model for a more balanced lifestyle. But the consensus among leaders of healthy Asian American congregations is that without that balance, the ministry will ultimately suffer more than it will benefit. "I'm seeing way too many unhealthy pastors who don't practice good self care," says ECC's Greg Yee. "Killing oneself and one's family in the name of ministry is never helping anybody."

The challenge for many Asian American pastors, particularly those in church plants, is that the work is endless, and there are many more opportunities to give of oneself than to receive. But healthy Asian American pastors know that they are setting an example for the rest of the church. "I have to be a Christian first as well as a dad and a husband, and people need to know that being a pastor isn't my whole life," says Ogimachi. "When you are in a church plant, you have diligent people who are usually willing to wear four or five hats; they are hard-working and sacrificial, but pastors have to watch to make sure they do not burn out. We must have an attitude where we accept our limitations rather than trying to be all things to all people."

Evergreen Baptist Church-LA's Fong believes that the process of setting boundaries is even more difficult in the Asian American setting, in part due to cultural influences such as being more community-oriented rather than individual-oriented. "In Asian American churches, we are really backward," he says.

> We don't encourage healthy boundary setting. People don't feel they can say no, they overextend themselves, and their lives are too fragmented and shallow because they've been taught it's unchristian to say no to teaching Sunday school when they're already doing three other things. Certainly the pastoral staff sets the stage for this. I have had to teach my congregation that it is OK to say no, even if it leaves our ministries short.

In healthy Asian American churches, key leaders not only model what it means to set appropriate boundaries in terms of balancing their lives, but they also try to ensure that their lay leaders and volunteers are striving for a similar balance to preserve the overall health of the congregation.

DEMONSTRATING VULNERABILITY

An emerging value for the current generation of Asian American church leaders, which was not considered or even desired by earlier generations, is demonstrating vulnerability. Interestingly, for male Asian American pastoral leaders who have not often seen this modeled in first generation pastors, a willingness to demonstrate vulnerability in public contexts has been a powerful way to connect with their postmodern congregations. "People really appreciate a sense of genuineness and vulnerability," says Open Door Presbyterian Church's Dihan Lee. "We've all seen and been burned by pastors who lead out of charisma and personality. When I talk to Asian Americans, I see people who are hungering for leaders who are real. Especially in Asian culture, it's difficult to express and be real about pain, but that's what the Asian American church needs."

In the process of planting Grace Community Covenant Church, senior pastor Steve Wong discovered that he had a tendency toward depression. Instead of hiding this from his congregation, he shared about it from the pulpit. "By doing so, it has helped to open the issue up for everyone in the church. They realize it's not something taboo or that can't be talked about," he says. "And if they're struggling with it, now they know there are resources, they can receive support, and it doesn't mean that something is bad about them. It takes some of the shame away. As a matter of integrity, I am trying not to segregate that part of my life from my leadership and from being a spiritual example to the church."

Having role models who are willing to share their struggles and challenges shatters the notion of the Christian leader as infallible and perfect, which is a different mentality from the way in which immigrant churches often viewed their senior leaders. However, this generation of both believers and nonbelievers already acknowledges and accepts the truth that all leaders have flaws, and they are looking for those who have the authenticity to share those weaknesses. "I make it a practice to share about my own doubts and struggles with my staff, my leaders and my congregation," says Fong. "Lately I've been making the point publicly that what qualifies me or anyone else to be in spiritual leadership is not that we are perfect but that we admit humbly needing to visit the cross daily."

When leaders do share more openly about their struggles, they create a safe haven that allows others in the congregation to do the same; the increased disclosure in a grace-filled community results in greater health within the congregation as a whole. But it must start with the leaders, who often find that in so sharing, they experience more blessing than they would have expected. Cambridge Community Fellowship Church's Soong-Chan Rah went through a rough period in his personal life when he struggled with his child's illness and his father's stroke. As he was preaching a sermon series on Isaiah, he found it easier to come up with questions rather than the answers. "Instead of glossing this over, I shared my struggles with the congregation. I shared that the answers from God were not as evident as they had

been in the past," he says. "Instead of any sort of condemnation, there was
a tremendous outpouring of support. Many remarked that this sermon was
one of my best, that it had the most impact. It was one of those times that I
felt confirmation that this was truly my church community, and not that I
was simply the pastor of the church."

VALUING TEAM MINISTRY

Healthy Asian American churches recognize that models in previous generations emphasizing hierarchy and authoritarian leadership do not work well
in the current context of post-first-generation Asian Americans living in a
postmodern society. As a result these congregations have chosen instead to
create more communal models of leadership that resonate with Asian American cultural tendencies as well as with current thinking on organizational
behavior. The old adage "two heads are better than one" succinctly explains
the value of teams that work well together: the synergies that result from
high-quality partnerships outweigh what one person can do alone. But there
are caveats to the adage, of which Asian American churches need to be
aware. One is that the two—or more—heads have to be in alignment with
and trusting of one another to ensure that synergy does occur. "A church
team cannot function well when all the members do not subscribe to the
same philosophy of ministry," says George Cladis. "This is one of the most
serious problems teams face."[10]

Team ministry does not mean that there are no levels of authority within
the team; in actuality, a healthy team will have a leader or leaders who can
guide the team and provide direction as well as making final decisions when
necessary. Asian American churches have sometimes executed the team-
ministry concept in a way that undermines its own progress by assuming
that it ultimately means achieving consensus on every point. "Although in
team ministry, everyone is equal before God, there are still differences in
roles," says David Gibbons.

Sometimes senior leaders will have to make decisions that are not popular with other leaders. Or you may have a majority of leaders who agree, but you don't have unanimity among your whole team. The key is to know how to handle these differences and still maintain a sense of unity. This takes a lot of wisdom. But not everyone will be a point leader on a team.

In fact, in the twenty-first-century church, having leaders who hone more specific gifts and abilities rather than trying to be a jack-of-all-trades may ultimately be more beneficial for a church. Open Door Presbyterian Church's senior pastor, Paul Kim, notes that "not all seminarians are going to become the head pastor or senior pastor of a congregation. So they have to know their strengths and specialize in that area rather than being a general practitioner. In the future, churches will be much more run in teams than by solo ministries." Today's healthy Asian American churches recognize the critical role that team ministry plays in their congregations and invest in the time and energy needed to make those teams work well.

RECOGNIZING GOD'S LEADERSHIP

Finally, the leaders of today's healthy Asian American congregations recognize that although they have been given responsibility for leadership within their churches, they must ultimately answer to their Leader and demonstrate the necessary humility and submission to God's headship as they strive to serve him. As Henri Nouwen discovered while ministering to the mentally handicapped at the L'Arche communities in Toronto, "I am getting in touch with the mystery that leadership, for a large part, means to be led."[11]

Grace May notes that particularly for Asian American church leaders, among whom there is a great propensity to seek people's approval, it is even more imperative that they bring themselves to the cross every day. "People pleasing is lethal in ministry," she says.

The way to combat that is to invest more time with God. That's the only way things can line up. God is the captain of the ship and the One who can still the seas. There will be storms and choppy waters, but

Jesus is the one who will help us stay the course. Because ultimately, ministry is not about making people followers of me, but followers of Christ.

Living under God's leadership as opposed to one's own provides the proper perspective and corrective for healthy Asian American church leaders. Fong says:

> Now that I'm getting close to fifty, I want the prize, which is to be able to stand before Christ and hear his affirmation of my life and my work. That means more to me than the affirmation of other people. I've told my congregation that I'm more dangerous now because I'm more concerned with pleasing God than with pleasing them. It's dreaming about becoming more and more the kind of church that really looks like Jesus, like the body of Christ.

BUILDING THE HOUSEHOLD OF GOD

Throughout this book, we have been using the image of a healthy household of God as a way to signify the desired ethos of today's Asian American churches. One significant challenge for these churches is not to confuse building a healthy *household* with building a healthy *house*. Many Asian American churches do a good job with building a seemingly healthy house of God. They have created the necessary ministries and functioning small groups; they tithe and give regularly; they have developed a well-oiled process for their Sunday services. However, building a healthy house just means that the church has a good public "face" that looks respectable from the outside. The question is whether that face is merely a façade housing a dysfunctional and ineffective household inside.

Building a healthy *household* has less to do with programs and ministries, and much more to do with the difficult task of creating strong, trusting relationships within the framework of the house. As any parent knows, maintaining and building high-quality relationships within a home takes a lifetime of investment, and it is no different in the spiritual realm of building a healthy household of God. The work that is often required to build a healthy household can't be measured in easily quantifiable ways, which makes it all the more difficult to do. Nor is there ever an end to the labor.

But current leaders of healthy Asian American households of God have committed themselves to practices and values that focus less on programs and processes, and more on the challenging but mission-critical aspects of leading, managing, and growing people—an approach that served Jesus quite well. Jesus focused his energies largely on developing his team of disciples, knowing that he would be able to reach the world by committing to just a finite few. In fact, he made a concerted effort to do more with less to maximize the Father's glory. Jesus didn't concern himself with programs or with the total number of his followers. He simply loved God and those God gave him to work with, teaching a small band of brothers how to do the same with one another. And that was enough to start the foundation of the universal household of God that, thousands of years later, is still growing and moving. Jesus serves as a good reminder for today's Asian American church leaders that the fruits of their labors may not be apparent until they are long gone, which is all the more reason to make sure that they are focusing their time and energies in the right places or, more accurately, in the right people.

5

TRUSTING HOUSEHOLDS

Openness to Change

JONATHAN WU

"WHY MESS UP A GOOD THING? You mean I will have to choose? How excruciating!"

I was serving as a pastoral intern at Evergreen Baptist Church of Los Angeles in 1995. I had the chance to work alongside some phenomenal leaders of what was regarded as a pillar Asian American congregation. Pastors Cory Ishida and Ken Fong had led a historic ethnic, immigrant, mainline denominational church to become a pioneering community that was pulsating with vitality and energy. And now the congregation was faced with a landmark decision. Whom would I follow?

BRIEF HISTORY OF EVERGREEN BAPTIST CHURCH OF LOS ANGELES

Evergreen Baptist Church was planted in 1925 by visionaries from the Los Angeles Baptist City Mission Society who reached out to first-generation Japanese Americans (*issei*). With subsequent generations experiencing the forced exodus of many during the internment of World War II and the gradual reentry afterward, this ethnic-specific faith community wrestled with the natural flow toward acculturation and assimilation into the wider American society. It began first with language. Some twenty-five years after its founding, Evergreen Baptist Church experienced its first significant change when the few remaining Japanese-speaking parents and grandparents created greater space and freedom for the growing, predominantly English-speaking younger generation by moving their worship service across the street. Although these two congregations remained in close proximity to each other, this marked a watershed moment in the ethos and direction of Evergreen Baptist Church.

The congregation came to the threshold of another critical juncture some twenty-five years later. Pastor Cory Ishida, the first third-generation Japanese American (*sansei*) to lead the church, attracted growing numbers of American-born Chinese who were drawn to his preaching and leadership. The church recognized this emerging trend by calling Ken Fong, a third-generation Chinese American, to become its first full-time associate pastor. The catalyst for a dynamic, increasingly more diverse ministry to English-speaking Asian Americans was now set in motion. God has richly blessed and empowered Evergreen Baptist Church in its most recent thirty years, stimulating creative thinking and innovative ministries to advance God's kingdom in the broader ethnic community.

By the early 1990s Evergreen Baptist Church had outgrown its church campus, drawing upwards of twelve hundred worshipers. Soon after, the church began to experience a gradual decline in Sunday attendance. The church felt big. People were comfortable and content. The search for a possibly larger church campus proved futile. Church leadership mused about possible alternatives. One emerged. Pastor Ishida felt God's prompting that the future of Evergreen would be best realized by forming two separate congregations with him and Pastor Fong leading as senior pastors of these respective churches. The initial reaction was shock and disbelief. Why make such a drastic change to the chemistry of Evergreen Baptist Church? Was it necessary? What if this decision backfired? This process of "hiving" into two churches would be difficult and painful. Friendships were stretched as individuals and families felt God's tugging to commit to and serve in different congregations. The breaking of the partnership between these two men felt to many like the divorce of one's own parents, where a child was forced to choose one over the other. The material assets of the church would also need to be divided equitably. Ministry leaders experienced the angst of separating from long-time colleagues and the anxiety of wondering who would step into those gaps. For others, the church "hive" created new opportunities and a sense of adventure. In the spring of 1997, Evergreen officially became two congregations, Evergreen Baptist Church of Los Angeles and Pastor Cory Ishida's new congregation, Evergreen Baptist Church of the San Gabriel Valley (Evergreen Baptist Church-SGV).

ENCOUNTERING CHANGE

Change is never easy and most often resisted. Yet it is also inevitable. Robert Quinn plainly expresses the options, "We would rather experience the pain of slow death than the threat of changing ourself."[1] Whether in a struggling congregation or a thriving church, people's reactions toward change are very similar. We don't like change. We are uncomfortable with what it might cost us. We are nervous about the uncertain future that may lie ahead. We would rather do nothing than embrace change. As the journey of Evergreen-LA revealed, however, we may have no choice. Time itself can provoke and instigate change. One might wish to maintain the status quo, but this is sometimes wishful thinking. Rather, one is confronted and challenged with a difficult choice. Weigh the prospects that change might bring or give oneself to the silent, almost imperceptible descent described by Quinn, that of slow death. A sign of health in emerging Asian American churches is the willingness to embrace and to learn and grow through change.

The story of waves and waves of Asian immigrants seeking a brighter future in the land of the Golden Mountain—this is how the Chinese have described America—mirrors the biblical narrative of the Hebrews of the Old Testament. The promise given to Abraham of a blessing was not only to be one of his own personal legacy but one of global consequence. He and his family were to uproot themselves and follow God to a new promised land,

and there his ancestors would be a divine blessing to the nations. Abraham's journey led him to Egypt, where generations that followed would settle down. But this was not really their home. Only later, when God would call on Moses to guide this incorrigible people from the comforts and security of this adopted, albeit foreign, residence toward their true, yet unknown destiny, would the first layer of God's promise see fulfillment. Throughout the Bible, we witness other examples of individuals and peoples who were reluctant and resistant to God's leading and directing. While there is always a biblical promise and hope, embracing change demands letting go of the familiar, safe, and sure.

For Evergreen, the motivations to engage change were both the logistical challenges on its facilities and a heightened sensitivity to spiritual stagnation within the congregation. Other congregations might face the departure of an influential leader or pastor. The church might struggle over preferred worship styles or the direction of its vision. Pastors and church leaders might battle over ministry priorities and stewardship of resources. The neighborhood around the church might undergo dramatic demographic transitions, raising concerns about personal safety and connectedness to the community. All congregations, whether they are first generation immigrant or moving toward a more diverse, multiethnic community, must wrestle with various kinds of difficulties and opportunities.

This chapter will present a biblical perspective on change, which can speak prophetically to Asian American church leaders and congregations who want to step courageously through change. It will also identify relevant cultural issues that must be considered in order to reduce the personal and corporate resistance to change and to increase the likelihood of a more positive outcome.

A BIBLICAL EPISODE ON CHANGE

As we reflect on the whole span of God's redemptive activity from Genesis through Revelation, we can see the seam of an unchanging eternal God breathing, moving and guiding dynamic change. From the initial downbeat of God's creative joy to ignite the whole universe into life to the grand finale of the new heaven and earth, we participate in a spectacular symphony of spiritual transformation.

This occurs both at the personal level as well as the collective realm. One has only to consider some of the significant biblical themes and motifs to understand that our openness to God's processes of spiritual change is embedded throughout. As we witness the wonder of God's transformational work in people, this requires an innate and willing disposition toward change. Pastor Erwin McManus puts it this way, "Repentance is change, conversion is change, regeneration is change, transformation is change, and sanctification is change. All of the deeply theological constructs that we have embraced and understand to be true cannot exist outside of a theology of change."[2] Welcoming God's initiatives in changing us more to the character and lifestyle of Jesus is normative for the Christian life and remains the leading edge toward deeper spiritual growth and maturity.

We also see how God's people are continually presented with situations involving change in order that they can more fully realize and participate in the profound mystery of God's purposes. The early church experienced this firsthand. Pentecost introduced Jews from all over the Diaspora to the irresistible gospel of the resurrected Christ. This drew scores of new converts into this tight-knit band of Jesus' followers. This infusion of people from various countries, with diverse cultural and language backgrounds, muddied the waters of the founding enclave. In Acts 6 it reached a crisis point when the Grecian Jews complained that their needy widows were being overlooked in the sharing of hospitality. This systemic challenge and its resolution greatly clarified the apostles' roles and responsibilities, and empowered others in the community to step into the new opportunities of ministry. Later on, the church encountered a far more serious issue: What is required to be a full-fledged member of the church? Non-Jews were being saved, finding their own indisputable place in the community and exercising their giftedness in service and leadership. Yet the Jewish majority refused to recognize God's sovereign activity. The tension as to whether the Gentile believers would be received into full fellowship was finally dealt with at the Council of Jerusalem (Acts 15), where the community finally acknowledged and affirmed that God's kingdom purposes must transcend personal preferences, ethnic heritage and cultural practices.

An invaluable yet critical resource in wrestling with the tensions that change invariably raises for individuals and congregations is the exercise of spiritual discernment. Change creates a pivot point; we can maintain the status quo by either doing nothing or very little, or cast a new trajectory by attempting something different. This becomes a fertile moment for seeking God's wisdom. Only as we submit to God's higher will and ways do we become more open to choosing the road much less traveled. Steve Wong, lead pastor of Grace Community Covenant Church in San Jose, California, took nine months to prepare his congregation for a key transition in their church life. Many new people had begun to visit the church. Their single service was reaching full capacity. The obvious solution was to launch a second service. This plan, however, was met with reluctance and resistance. Current members expressed concern that the children's ministry programs would not be adequately staffed and that the tight family community they had experienced and valued would be lost. The leadership paused and facilitated many discussions within the congregation. All were invited to pray over this decision. Ultimately, the congregation needed to embrace and own the decision that the doors to Grace Community would remain open to those outside this household of God. This was eventually affirmed by all. Further, the leadership team demonstrated foresight by keeping this change as a short-term test, subject to evaluation six months later. This openness to listen and learn together gave permission for continuing dialogue and future modifications and improvements. Change is best managed when the people of God listen, pray and work together to discern God's guidance and leading.

NOT WORTH THE RISKS

People are seldom naturally inclined toward change. They prefer to keep thing as they are. If nothing's wrong, why disturb the peace? Especially since change is risky. Our congregations likewise generally seek to avoid or delay the need for change. It can create chaos. It can upset the sense of harmony. Since change can rarely guarantee positive outcomes at the outset, people most often feel that it is not worth the risk.

Churches typically are seen as conservative institutions. People self-select a congregation because it best matches or reflects their theological persuasion, social needs or personal preferences. And as this happens the culture and ethos of these fellowships can become more reinforced, making them more impervious to change. Denominational churches, with their staunch adherence to traditions and practices, may find it difficult to attract new congregants or incorporate new models of ministry. Megachurches, often initiated as change movements, might find themselves staggering to keep up with the perpetual demands for spiritual goods and services from their constituents. Subsequently, these congregations may need to slow their drive to innovate just to create equilibrium and establish stability for the sake of their people. In a similar way, many first-generation faith communities may dread the prospects of imminent change as they assimilate further into the multiethnic world in America.

Asian congregations frequently began as gathering places for recent immigrants. They emerged in concentrated demographic pockets like Koreatown or Little Saigon. They formed from small groups of international students who finished their academic studies, found work, started families and strengthened relational networks with other postgraduate peers. Other Asians, Christian or not, were drawn to these fellowships because a common language was spoken, food was recognizable and they felt comfortable, at home. These churches frequently served as community centers. Business, social and spiritual interests commingled, forging a vibrant and vital haven where fewer barriers needed to be crossed and where one felt at ease. The relentless feeling of being alone and a stranger here in America provided additional incentive for our first-generation Asian sisters and brothers to gravitate toward shared life together.

But, as is seen in many of our Asian churches, the children and grandchildren of the faithful adult believers discover that their own spiritual journey may lead them away from their familial roots. Many factors contribute to this. College either deepens their Christian faith as they participate in campus ministries like InterVarsity Christian Fellowship, or it releases them from the reaches of their parents' faith. They may have grown weary of being consistently reminded that they are children in their parents' church. They may be tired of in-church politics and conflict. They may simply feel the more immediate interest of connecting with their peers. None of these factors should be viewed as negative or critical of how they were shaped and influenced in their younger years. They merely indicate the possible causes of a silent exodus from the Asian immigrant church. Evergreen Baptist Church-LA and other emerging Asian American and multiethnic churches have welcomed many college and young adults who were raised and nurtured in these immigrant congregations. But is there anything their home congregations can do or could have done to serve them better or retain them longer? This demographic transition is just one example of what our congregations may face and where risk-taking is critical for long-term vitality.

The willingness and courage to engage in change requires risk: the risk of trying something and then falling on one's face; the risk of raising hopes and expectations and then disappointing others or becoming disillusioned oneself; the risk of gaining nothing except pain, headaches, and an aversion to risk again. Change is costly. And change, or even its remote possibilities, can feel threatening to a culture that prides itself on cohesiveness, continuity and stability.

For many Asians, whether South Asian Indians, Japanese, Koreans, Chinese or others, we are blessed with a history rich in tradition and culture. This legacy is captured in our classical arts and literature. It is evident in how we talk about our family trees. It is seen in how we honor our elders. It is very evident in how we hold on to language and cultural practices that remind us of our ethnic background. The Asian church not only gathers many who are drawn by their shared cultural heritage but also, in many ways, allows these ways to continue to be perpetuated, honored and retained. The strength of our cultural heritage, then, can become a significant hindrance in taking the necessary steps to adapt to and participate more fully in our North American context.

Many Asian churches place high regard on the family. Because the family is the primary social network, Asian congregations can often be seen as an extension of that relational system. It remains common that individuals are known by their last names. Sometimes close adult friends are called "Uncle" or "Auntie" by the children. Shared meals (e.g., lunch after worship service) or communal events (e.g., an all-church retreat) provide the social time for networking with one's spiritual clan. In some cases the senior pastor becomes a spiritual father figure, making decisions affecting the household. These all reinforce a prevailing feeling of being part of a unique, extended family. Clear identification of a person's role provides sanctuary for his or her sense of self. Knowing this, any decision or action that might disrupt the harmony and the peace of the family might be resisted or suppressed.

Individual and corporate shame can be another significant hindrance toward stepping into the waters of change. Questioning those in leadership positions may cause them to seek to preserve public face. It may also put the questioner in the awkward posture of being seen as a troublemaker. Even as Asian culture and Asian churches value relational harmony, possible change can escalate a heightened sense of fear—fear of embarrassment, fear of standing out and alone, fear of failing and disappointing others, fear of inflicting more harm than producing benefit and good. Even as there is much to celebrate and to affirm about the value and commitment to family in Asian American life and culture, we must also recognize its shadow side: it may stymie necessary growth and change.

The image of the household of God is an extremely vivid and powerful way of inviting Asian American congregations to greater health. We recognize that we all serve the same sovereign and good God, our heavenly Father, who is redeeming all of human life and bringing together a new family. We join the works of Jesus Christ and the Holy Spirit as we are called to partner in God's kingdom activity. Scripture becomes our common guide to know the mind and heart of God and to practice our biblical convictions. Community is the gathering of spiritual brothers and sisters, families and singles, old and young to a place where we learn how to serve and love one another. From our corporate solidarity with God and one another comes the courage and resolve to press through change, whether casual or drastic. That is the beginning of building the necessary trust to move toward positive change.

TRUST FACTOR

The most important commodity in change dynamics is trust. People are most open to influence and action when they are strengthened in their faith in God and in God's good purposes for them, and when they have confidence in those who are leading them. For some, however, this may not be their church experience. They have seen leaders act autocratically. They have had to go through divisions or even splits because irreconcilable factions emerged. They may have been confused or angered by the lack of spiritual integrity of their pastors or elders. All of this reinforces the critical need for trust and for confidence in God and those God has appointed to lead and shepherd these congregations.

Asian American congregations can face corporate change in a healthy manner when they anchor this process in a strong trust in God and what God is doing in their churches. We, as members of God's household, can know that God passionately loves the church and will fulfill God's purposes through us. How we see God and our confidence in God's good character is instrumental in forming a positive attitude toward change. This, in fact, can ultimately stem the tide of people's fear and insecurity, and build the necessary momentum toward deeper faith and courage. Wayne Ogimachi thought that he would stay in Berkeley, California, for many more years. He had invested much in his church and had seen the spiritual fruit in his people. But God had new plans for him and his family—starting a new church in Seattle, Washington. Lighthouse Christian Church was birthed. Now in its fourth year and reaching many unchurched Asian Americans, Ogimachi looked back and commented, "I felt in my heart, I am content where I am. If it weren't for God's call, I would not even consider this option. After I made the change, I realized I needed to make a change, but I didn't know that I did. After I made it, this was true." When God moves in the hearts and minds of key leaders, they can become a very necessary influence and source of confidence for the congregation.

Healthy Asian American congregations become more receptive to change when they trust their spiritual leaders. Prior to the long tenures of Pastor Cory Ishida and now Pastor Ken Fong, Evergreen Baptist Church-LA was similar to many Asian churches. Pastors came and left. Sometimes they were called to other places of ministry. Other times their departures were on less cordial terms. This continual pattern of leadership turnover heightened a growing sense of instability and declining morale for this small Japanese congregation. All they wished for was someone to be their pastor and to stay with them. In 1977 the faithful remnant of thirty some members approached Cory Ishida, a young youth pastor, who had yet to go to seminary for formal training. They liked his very simple strategy to revitalize the church—preach the Word and pray. He agreed to be their shepherd and then remained with them for the next twenty years. When Evergreen Baptist Church-LA decided to hive into two congregations in 1997, the church family could face this dramatic decision because Ishida had cared for his congregation for such a significant period of time. They trusted God's leading through him and Fong. This was so critical to address lingering doubts, reluctance or resistance. The high level of congregational confidence in their spiritual leaders was one of the most significant reasons why this change was able to proceed as well as it did. Churches that recognize the trustworthiness of their God-given leaders and take to heart God's leading through these people are better prepared to engage in significant corporate change.

There are many ways church leaders can gain the confidence and trust of their people. One is to lead by personal example. Congregations are more willing to follow when their leaders set the pace. Change is nothing new for NewSong Church in Irvine, California. Started by lead pastor David Gibbons from the living room of his family's apartment, NewSong Church was used to being stretched as they grew in and out of various worship sites. Through all of these challenges, the congregation grew in number and faith. Yet unexpected circumstances would directly challenge Gibbons and his leadership team about the future direction of their ministry. A homeless person began living in a shed on their church property, and the staff prodded the pastor to decide what they should do. He realized that God was putting the concern for misfits and the marginalized in his face. He could have avoided or been apathetic to the situation, but he recognized that this had something to do with the heart of God. Gibbons said, "There has to be personal buy-in. If I'm going to be real about this, I have to give to this. I had to change my schedule. I had to devote 10% of my time to this cause." So he and the NewSong Church staff spent six months wrestling with the issue of social justice. They led the congregation through a sobering study of the Scriptures on God's heart for the poor. The staff walked the streets of impoverished neighborhoods right near the church. Gibbons became personally involved with several compassion organizations, including World Vision. These all solidified his conviction and NewSong Church's commitment for seizing God's cause of justice, advocacy and compassion. People will go where their leaders have gone. They will be more willing to go through change as they witness their leaders being transformed and changed.

Building the social capital of trust is vitally important in Asian American congregations. Because the life and activities of the church are centered on relationships, positive and healthy interaction, genuine and authentic commitment to each other, and confidence in one's leaders will greatly improve the prospects for successful change. The ethos of change is best cultivated when there is an abundance of trust, which provides the strength and perseverance to weather the uncertainties that a new spiritual direction or movement will bring. Congregations who have faith in God and in those whom God has raised to lead and guide them have taken a very significant step toward building the critical momentum toward embracing change. However, this journey toward change cannot be an individual initiative; it must become a collective commitment to learning and growing through this process.

FOSTERING A DISCERNING COMMUNITY

"The nail that sticks up is hammered down." This Japanese proverb aptly summarizes the general feeling about experiencing change within the context of a community. If an individual decides to step forward and change, the surrounding system, whether it is family, ethnic community or church, may quickly intervene to restore conformity and a sense of harmony. For change to effectively take hold, there must be a shared commitment by all to enter its murky water and covenant to stay together no matter the outcome. A community that changes starts with being a community that learns and discerns together.

One extremely beneficial condition in preparing and strengthening a congregation to walk through change is that the whole church, leaders and members, are willing to be a community of discernment. This brings those entrusted with spiritual authority to collaborate and share the process of engaging in corporate change with the larger congregation. Discernment invites the whole community to listen to God, to each other and to the unique context and setting of their ministry focus. This will enable them to discover more of God's intentions and purposes, identify and celebrate their unique congregational strengths and become energized and empowered to hear and pursue God's calling on their life and mission together. Working through the change process can be a very fertile season of deep learning and insight for all who participate. The genuine health of a congregation is not primarily evaluated on the basis of what it accomplishes or how much it achieves, but more so on who they are becoming and how they feel about that transformational process and about their community. Peter Cha, professor of pastoral theology at Trinity Evangelical Divinity School, comments, "When churches more and more embrace this concept, we are not only worshiping communities, we're not just missional communities, but we're also learning communities; it paves the way for all kinds of changes."

Because change is a very dynamic process, congregations must be attentive to the movement of God's Spirit in guiding and shaping their priorities and activities. Paul Kim, senior pastor of Open Door Presbyterian Church in Herndon, Virginia, has witnessed numerous examples in which his first-generation Korean American church took to heart God's purpose for their congregation, but one such example stands out. Almost ten years ago Kim felt that a major stumbling block to the continued growth of the church he served was its name, Korean Orthodox Presbyterian Church. This posed several different yet equally formidable barriers for non-Koreans to feel welcomed and accepted. It framed a very narrow doorway of entry. So he began to plant the seed of modifying the church name. He shared it with his staff and elder board. He consistently wove variations of this thought in his messages. He highlighted the importance of God's global mission to all peoples. Kim reflected back, "The more drastic the change, the longer it takes. You have to be patient." The breakthrough took place only after a key leader of the church, and one who was opposed to the name change, returned from a summer mission project totally transformed and now himself convinced that God's mission should supersede maintaining an exclusive posture on the ethnic identity of the church. Seven years after Paul first planted this idea, the congregation finally adopted its new name. The pathway toward a strong church formation and identity will rarely be straightforward and direct. By acknowledging a dependence on God's leading and affirming a growing trust in those God has given spiritual authority, congregations can navigate the challenges of growing together through change.

What marks a church as a discerning community? It begins with the pastor and other key leaders acknowledging and expressing their commitment to learn and to be shaped with the congregation. It is equally critical that people sense that those whom they have given the charge of spiritual responsibility are receptive and responsive to the leading of God through others.

Evergreen Baptist Church-LA faced many difficult circumstances after the "hive." Fong remembers looking out at his new congregation and realizing that he did not recognize many of those who stayed at the "old" site. The church board had many new leaders. The various ministries were scrambling to identify and train new volunteers. The church had a mixed financial picture. They had a building that had no outstanding debt, but they also had a very thin cash reserve in their bank account. And the church had to deal with a pressing issue about their facilities. The city had granted several extensions on a decision concerning whether to remove portable trailers on the church property or to convert them into permanent structures. These had adequately served the needs of the children and youth ministries. But now the city wanted a final answer. The church senior leadership faced several difficult choices. They could shore up the temporary facilities, which had a very short future. Or they could consider building a permanent but far more costly ministry center. The church board brought this matter to the membership. The final decision was given to the church members. Both options had their benefits and costs.

What was God inviting the church to become through this season of faith and courage? After serious discussions and considerable prayer, the congregation decided to go ahead and embark on a capital campaign just months after the historic hive. The people's discerning of God's voice was affirmed three years later, when they were not only able to enjoy a brand-new facility for their children and youth, but they also celebrated the paying off of the entire project debt. Through this faith journey, the church family was both inspired and revitalized.

A learning community forges more than a wider shared ownership in any process of congregational change. It can also deepen and refine the inner character of the church family. Cambridge Community Fellowship Church, near Boston, constantly deals with change. Attracting students from the many nearby colleges and universities, Cambridge must manage the stress of continual turnover of its young congregation. Yet because of his intense convictions on social justice and multiethnicity, senior pastor Soong-Chan Rah wanted his congregation to grapple more intentionally and deeply with how they were going to live out their vision and values. What does it mean to be a multiethnic community? What does it mean to pursue God's heart for social justice? He formed a small learning community of pastoral staff and key leaders to brainstorm these issues and to grow together. They read *Divided by Faith,*[3] a seminal critique on the state of racial reconciliation in American evangelical church life. They heard about and shared in each other's personal journeys. They engaged in serious dialogue about their church's vision, values, practices and activities. They reviewed their findings with the congregation. And this learning community process presses forward even now. Rah shared, "The most significant benefit was the process of the team experience."

As Asian American congregations stretch forward to contribute to the wider kingdom activity of the church, they can become exemplary models of faithful and faith-filled communities by seeking to know and follow God's will together. Cha adds, "When the senior pastor listens to others, he models the learning community that is a more communal experience. When that happens, the congregation is less resistant to change. Learning provokes change. The byproduct of a learning community is transformation." Indeed, the promise of future strategic contributions of many healthy and vibrant Asian American churches emerges out of an intentional commitment to corporate discernment, learning and action.

LEADING CHANGE

Healthy emerging Asian American churches are discerning communities that energetically participate in and experience ongoing transformation. The entire congregation discovers more of who they are and what God desires for them. While all share in the journey of change, the responsibility for leading this process rests primarily with church leaders. What should elders, pastors and other leaders keep in mind as they prepare their people for change? Let me suggest several critical factors.

Any change process begins with a *definite need*. People will not change unless there is a compelling motivation to do so. And there are many barriers and limiting forces to thwart the progress toward change. There is the fear of the unknown, the fear of instability, reluctance to risk and resistance to let go. Leaders must assess and determine whether God is preparing the community for possible change and transformation.

Leaders should take sufficient time to consider whether initiating change is *appropriate for that particular season* of their church's life. A qualitative and quantitative congregational assessment can provide important information to the leaders on the prevailing attitudes, opinions and feelings among the people. Attention should be given to not only the congregation's spiritual and emotional conditions of a readiness but also the physical, historical and social character. Leaders can prepare well for change by being astute and careful observers of the congregation's openness to God's work in their individual and corporate life, their personal feelings about the church, and their level of enthusiasm and excitement in worship and ministry.

In addition, equal attention might be given to other perspectives on community life. What has happened in the recent history of the church that can either advance or hinder change? What is the quality of relationships within the congregation? Is there good communication and trust between leaders and church members? Has there been a noticeable increase in interpersonal conflict, grumbling or discontent? What is the church's financial status? Responses to these and other questions can enlighten and inform the leaders about the well-being and fitness of the church and how it might respond to change.

The example of Evergreen Baptist Church's experience of church hiving is indeed remarkable. Not many congregations, Asian or otherwise, would embark on such a radical change. The adventure from one mature congregation into two thriving communities encompassed nearly two years of prayer, thoughtful deliberation and intentional planning. The senior leaders did their very best to care for and guide the church family. A transition team, led by Pastor Arlene Inouye, outlined and executed a thoughtful process of moving people deeper with God and with each other in order to more fully prepare and equip the congregation. They addressed organizational and ministry development issues as well as the personal and corporate readiness of the church family. The team developed timely sermon series that acknowledged and addressed the real and felt needs of the people. People were given opportunity to listen and respond to the voice of God both individually and corporately. Leadership teams for the two churches were organized, and significant time was given for relationship building, vision sharing and strategic planning. To prepare for the eventual separation of friends, ministry colleagues and the larger church family, the transition team developed a Bible study series on affirmation, healing and reconciliation. These studies recognized that what mattered most was not future missional opportunities of the two churches but the genuine character and authentic relationships of all the people. This congregational journey culminated in a closing celebration that remembered God's grace and goodness to the united Evergreen family throughout its history.

Successful change also builds from an increased *sense of urgency*. Pastors and ministry leaders must persuasively communicate that the time to consider change is now. Robert Quinn states, "It is much easier and safer for us to stay within the zone of certainty, particularly if we are mired in the slow death dilemma and suffering. The challenges arise as we contemplate deep change. We must reach a point of ultimate despair and frustration before we seriously think about initiating deep change."[4] While we might not want to paint such a grave picture to our congregation, sometimes they must feel the weight of what doing nothing might mean. A famous Chinese proverb states, "If one must suffer, it is much better to shorten the pain." John Kotter has written, "Major change is never successful unless the complacency level is low. A high urgency rate helps enormously in completing all the stages of a transformation process."[5] As has been captured by the various stories of Asian American congregations in this chapter, courage to step into the unpredictable waters of change, to accept the consequences of risk-taking and to be prompted by a divine sense of urgency can result in a significant experience of corporate renewal and revitalization of vision and purpose.

Openness to change is also enhanced by *a compelling vision*. While some in our congregations may react to the threats of pain and suffering, more of our people respond and are more motivated by a clear and inspirational purpose for personal and corporate change. This is the critical role of vision formation. Ogimachi of Lighthouse Christian Church has remarked, "Change works best when it is built on the mission and vision of the church. Rather than just emphasizing what is new, help people see how the proposed change extends the values of the past." Change should connect with God's vision for the congregation. As earlier congregational stories indicate, the fear of change can be addressed by the reminder of our confidence in God, God's mission for the church, and the unique passion and gifts that God has given to a particular congregation. Each church has the ever-present potential to be shaped by vision and to do something special about it. Ray Rood, a strategic-planning consultant and the president of Human Technologies International, has developed a useful model of approaches toward the future. He describes that most organizations and leaders see the future and merely react to it. Others may pause and then respond to the prospect ahead of them. Some will seize the opportunity and be proactive. Yet few will look ahead and seek to invent and create the future as if it has already taken place. This is the power of vision casting and of reshaping and reforming the culture of a congregation to believe that it can take its future into its own hands.

Sustaining successful change may also require creating and celebrating intermediate goals that can be achieved; these will encourage progress toward the longer-term goals and objectives. Frequently the target may be incredibly ambitious, and a congregation may buckle with some internal fears of failure. However, if some more modest steps can be taken, the successful collaborative experience will strengthen the community's enthusiasm and resolve, ownership will increase and momentum will be sustained.

CULTIVATING THE RIGHT ETHOS FOR CHANGE

Since the hive in 1997, Evergreen Baptist Church-LA and Evergreen Baptist Church-SGV continue to flourish in their ministry to Asian Americans as well as to the ethnically diverse population in the Los Angeles area. Evergreen Baptist Church-SGV has planted two additional churches to reach unchurched Asian Americans. It has attracted large numbers of families through its expansive sports ministry and is nurturing hundreds of children through its Sunday school program. Fong has led Evergreen Baptist Church-LA to recast its vision to become an emerging missional church, where the increasingly ethnically heterogeneous congregation is testifying to and reflecting Jesus' passion for reconciliation. The church has grown twofold and many young people have been drawn to its dynamic worship services and church ministries. As church leaders and the core community of the two Evergreen Baptist churches look back, they truly believe that through this church hive, God sovereignly led and prepared them for something far greater than they could have imagined.

Through the stories of Asian American congregations we have discovered some useful reminders of how strategic change can be initiated, prepared for, followed through and established in the life of emerging Asian American churches.

First, a congregation must begin by understanding God's purpose for the church and appreciating the more unique calling and priorities for its particular community. No two churches are completely alike. God has formed and shaped each to identify, pursue and fulfill its special place in the wider mission of the kingdom of God. Change for the sake of change or for the purpose of imitating another church's experiences and success does not accomplish what God would seek for God's people. God has had a very significant role for the immigrant congregation, a front-door outreach to first-generation Asians. God has equally given Asian American and multiethnic churches opportunities to further God's redemptive and reconciling work in our increasingly diverse society. God will forge new models of fellowships and churches that will advance God's eternal purposes beyond this generation's aspirations and dreams. Our work as agents of change and transformation begins with embracing God's heart for the world and being open to participate with God however God leads.

Second, a congregation must be given sufficient time to cultivate the right ethos and prospects for positive change. The spiritually attentive leader will benefit from learning about the history of change in the church. The perceptive pastor will assess and discern the overall health and readiness of the congregation to step out in faith with courage. The wise elder will be quick to listen, slow to speak and compassionately empathize with the concerns and fears of the people. But most important, the integrity of the spiritual leaders is critical in preparing and creating the fertile soil for change.

Third, congregational openness to change is greater when leaders develop a comprehensive yet flexible process. The course toward corporate transformation and systemic change can never be fully charted or anticipated. It requires a spirit of humility, patience and perseverance to sustain the desired objectives as well as to support and love the people affected by change. Arlene Inouye, who served as the pastor of discipleship ministries at the time of Evergreen Baptist Church's hive, has succinctly synthesized several key ingredients regarding change in the church.

- Initiation. The change is initiated by God and discerned through prayer. Prayer is imperative throughout the change process.

- Identification. Key goals, issues, people, questions and potential problems are identified, and plans and strategies are developed in light of change and in line with the church's vision. The articulation of concrete results is helpful.

- Inquiry. An inquiry and assessment tool (survey, needs assessments, etc.) is used to reveal where people and the ministry are.

- Invitation. People are invited to actively participate in the change process, with their input and feedback seriously considered.

- Information. People are well informed regarding the possibility, process and progress of change, not simply of decisions made.

- Implementation. Responsibility for the implementation of plans is designated (preferably to a team of both staff and lay people) with plans (subject to modifications) that are clear and doable. The plans are comprehensive and holistic in nature, addressing spiritual, emotional/psychological, relational as well as organizational issues and factors.

- Influence. Staff and lay leaders influence the church family with wisdom and sensitivity under the guidance of the Holy Spirit. Unity, even if not uniformity of opinion, is important.

Envisioning and experiencing congregational change can be an intimidating process. So much is not fully known. There are the genuine prospects of disappointment, frustration or disillusionment. We can see failed change as a personal and collective setback. And yet we are invited to witness God's sovereign and good work in many Asian American churches. These transformational opportunities will be bold initiatives of community faith and perseverance. They will build legacies of maturing trust and confidence in God and those God places in spiritual leadership. They will bring people together toward a common purpose and mission. They will revitalize and energize the local church to further pursue God's call on their life together. Being open and receptive to God's work of transformation and change is both critical and beneficial to the future health and vitality of Asian American and multiethnic congregations.

6

HOSPITABLE HOUSEHOLDS

Evangelism

HELEN LEE

FOR A GLIMPSE INTO WHAT THE FUTURE of the Asian American church may hold, look no further than Nicole Gon, a twenty-three-year-old, fourth-generation Chinese and Japanese American who lives in Southern California and attends Evergreen Baptist Church of Los Angeles. In addition to her own multiethnic heritage as a tricultural American, she represents a new and emerging category of Asian American Christian: those who are discovering new ways to pursue evangelism that focus less on programs than on living a lifestyle that draws people to Jesus.

Attracted to Evergreen Baptist Church-LA by its emphasis on social justice, Gon found others at the church who shared her interest in community development, particularly for the lower-income areas of Los Angeles. She began living with other women from the church in their twenties who all had the same desire to influence a local community and bring the love of Christ to their neighbors, which they accomplished by building relationships with neighboring families, tutoring local children, taking prayer walks and planning regular meetings together. "We've gotten particularly close to two families," Gon says. "One is from Mexico, the other from China. There is sometimes such diversity around our dinner table when we're eating with our neighborhood friends, because I'm Asian and my roommate is white, yet we all get along."

Although it may appear that progress has been slow in that Gon has not yet seen any dramatic conversions take place, she has experienced growth in unexpected ways since she began living in the lower-income neighborhood of Rosemead. "My personal growth has been tremendous. Even more than doing ministry, living in community has really taught me how to raise issues with people and to reconcile with them," she says.

Gon has also discovered that her attitudes about evangelism are changing. "Now when I meet people I don't think that my sole goal is to convert them. I've realized that it takes a really long time for that to happen. So now I seek to love my neighbors as I get to know and serve them. Making them Christians is not my sole motive."

■ ■ ■

The word *evangelism* doesn't appear anywhere in the Bible. You can find the Greek words *euangelion,* meaning "good news" or *euangelistēs,* meaning "evangelist," numerous times in the Scriptures; however, *evangelism* is a word that has emerged over time, a word intended to describe the process and programs of today's Christians as they share the good news of Jesus Christ. In contrast, the early church never seemed to concern itself with how to "do evangelism." For these Christians evangelism was a way of life, not an obligation or a task relegated only to those who consider themselves evangelists. The early church knew that their good news had to be shared, even if it meant death. For them evangelism was woven into the fabric of their being as Christ followers.

Today's healthy Asian American churches are beginning to reclaim the heritage of the early church by focusing on their communities and building on existing relationships to change hearts and souls for Christ. Their new approaches bode well for the future, because many of the modern evangelistic approaches have not been effective in reaching unchurched or previously churched Asian Americans living in a postmodern age. Instead, these churches think of evangelism not as a program but as a way of life that proclaims the good news to those who have open hearts, souls and minds.

In this chapter, we will first review a number of Asian American cultural tendencies that create a lens through which churches need to view their evangelistic efforts. Next, we will examine several key biblical and theological principles of evangelism that are particularly relevant for Asian American churches. Last, we will look at the ways that today's healthy Asian American churches are living out the Great Commission in their churches.

ASIAN AMERICAN CULTURE: HOW IT HELPS AND HINDERS EVANGELISM

Strong community orientation (vs. individualism). In 1903 the first Korean immigrants, one hundred workers destined for sugarcane farms, landed on the shores of Hawaii, which began a wave of migration that continues to the present. The Korean newcomers found refuge and strength in church, which they created on their arrival. A century later more than 4,000 Korean churches exist in the United States, but the growth in the number of these churches has had little to do with any targeted evangelistic effort from any one particular ministry body or organization. Church provided not only spiritual support and relational fellowship, but also gave the new immigrants resources to help with basic needs such as food, money and job support. In addition, the church became the overriding institution that helped Koreans maintain their own cultural identity. Korean churches in America grew largely because of the relationships that the immigrants formed with one another to buttress themselves against the stresses and challenges of being in a strange land.

Even without the added pressures of immigrant life, these Korean and other Asian immigrants have perpetually demonstrated a key cultural trait that is equally present in later generations of Asian Americans today: an emphasis on community. This relational focus is one differentiating factor between Asian Americans and other parts of the church family in the United

States—and it has an impact on how effective evangelism is done in Asian American churches.

"The first generation culture was very kinship oriented," says Soong-Chan Rah, senior pastor of Cambridge Community Fellowship Church of Cambridge, Massachusetts. "The way evangelism was done in those contexts was very relational. For example, it was about one Korean immigrant asking another to church. This is a very positive legacy we have received from our parents."

For today's Asian American Christians this relational emphasis permeates their lives and, by extension, their choices and preferences with regard to their church. They look for churches that demonstrate the importance of community, whose members assist one another in tangible, concrete ways and, more importantly, whose relationships reflect healthy attitudes and practices. As a result, healthy Asian American churches have understood the importance of this cultural trait and have built churches with a strong emphasis on high-quality community.

For most Asian American churches effective marketing usually has nothing to do with traditional business methods. "You can advertise all you want in the newspapers, but Asian Americans are not going to be drawn to that," says Steve Wong, lead pastor of Grace Community Covenant Church in Los Altos, California. "Asian Americans have to find out about a church through people they know." In other words, effective marketing occurs through the Asian American grapevine, a very community-oriented approach befitting the target audience's cultural tendencies.

Relational dysfunctions. Yet despite the high value that Asians generally place on family and relationships, Asian Americans grapple with the challenge of living a bicultural life, and perhaps the most significant area in which these tensions manifest themselves is within the family. Due to communication difficulties, cultural differences and too-high expectations from their parents, Asian immigrant children may have contentious, troubled or strained relationships with their mother and father. Then they often bring the same patterns of communication into their own marital and peer relationships. This history and pattern of relational dysfunction can have a significant effect in the church context, particularly with regard to evangelistic efforts. The danger is that today's postmodern pre-Christians and non-Christians are sensitive to relational disharmony, and when they see or experience unresolved tensions and conflicts in a church, they are apt to go elsewhere to find the community and authenticity they seek—and there is no guarantee that they will look to another church to find that community.

In Asian culture, conflict is usually evidence that one party has done something wrong, and thus conflict is typically avoided at all costs. Instead, both parties try to preemptively find the correct way to behave and then act accordingly to prevent conflict. But in a Westernized culture such as the United States, conflict is seen as a natural byproduct of bringing a group of individuals together. Thus conflict is inevitable and natural, something that can't be avoided. Because of the difference between what many Asian Americans have grown up experiencing in their families versus what they experience in the Western context, the area of conflict resolution is a significant challenge in the church. "Asian Americans generally do not know how to do healthy relationships, especially conflict resolution," says David Gibbons, senior pastor of NewSong Church in Irvine, California. "But the test of our authentic relationships is how we handle conflict." So healthy Asian American churches rise to the challenge of dealing with conflict, continuing to promote and build healthy relationships that ultimately serve as a significant evangelistic draw.

Churches with healthy communities are attractive to the postmodern generation because they see people speaking the truth to one another in love and that conflict is dealt with in a mature and healthy way. That type of authenticity, which can be so difficult to find in an Asian American context, has become a drawing point in healthy Asian American churches.

Resistance to "losing face." Although relationships are highly valued by Asian Americans, a key barrier to living in authentic and genuine relationship is the Asian need to "preserve face." This means avoiding situations that could result in bringing shame or discomfort upon oneself or one's family.

In the area of evangelism, Asian Americans often find themselves feeling inadequate or insecure about how to reach nonbelievers, and as a result they avoid interactions with seekers or nonbelievers that may result in an uncomfortable situation.

Instead, once Asian Americans find people with whom they feel comfortable in church, they have difficulty breaking out of those comfort zones. Wayne Ogimachi, pastor of Lighthouse Christian Church of Issaquah, Washington, notes that in Asian culture, it is often unnatural to introduce oneself to another person. "There's a little voice in my mind that says, *Why would a stranger want to know me?*" he says. "I think often in Asian American churches, we are cliquish not because we're unfriendly but because we don't know how to talk to someone we don't know. We have to wait until somebody introduces us first." In other words, too much "face" is at stake to speak with either church newcomers or unchurched Asian Americans.

Another area in which saving face affects evangelistic efforts is in the Asian American avoidance of situations that require relational risk-taking. "Asian Americans tend to be a little bit on the passive side," says Rah. "I'm not the type of person to go knocking on doors. Most Asian Americans are like that. We are not the aggressive, conversation-starter types. We have a degree of timidity."

Even for those Asian Americans who feel they have built strong relationships with others, the relationships can be limited in depth because many Asian Americans lack role models who have demonstrated vulnerability and openness with their struggles and weaknesses. The Asian cultural emphasis on keeping proper "face" can hinder Asian American Christian growth by maintaining the right exterior—the right job, the right house, the right education—rather than revealing an interior life that might be characterized by more wrongs than rights.

Gibbons notes, "We're a shame-based culture. Our cultural tendency is to keep our struggles inside, which is a major hurdle. But transparency was Jesus' way. Purity is about openness before God."

As a result, Asian Americans will either have to find ways to suppress their natural inclination to avoid situations that might naturally feel uncomfortable when it comes to reaching nonbelievers, or they will have to find alternative ways of interacting with nonbelievers that meshes well with their native tendencies.

RELEVANT BIBLICAL AND THEOLOGICAL PRINCIPLES FOR TODAY'S ASIAN AMERICAN CHURCHES

Healthy Asian American churches will keep in mind cultural influences as they build the strategies and programs for their churches. But at the same time they know their approach must be shaped by more than just Asian culture. In fact, these churches recognize that it is most important to stay focused on biblical and theological principles to ground their evangelism—in particular, principles that have special relevance for Asian American congregations.

ACKNOWLEDGE GOD'S LOVE FOR THE "OUTSIDER"

Ken Fong, senior pastor of Evergreen Baptist Church-LA, uses the metaphor of adoption in his book *Secure in God's Embrace*. "To truly understand God's love," Fong writes, "you will have to think of yourself as a spiritual orphan and of God as a loving father intent on adopting as many orphaned children as possible into his family."[1]

Although it is certainly true that all people are made in God's image and may claim him as their Father, Fong's adoption analogy may have particular relevance for Asian Americans. The idea of belonging to a family is one that resonates deeply within the Asian American heart. But even though Asian American churches are often characterized by strong community, this sometimes results in a weakness in reaching beyond the community to outsiders.

This also was a challenge for the earliest Christians. One of the biggest paradigm shifts they had to make was to understand that Jesus died not just for the Jews but for the world. To make the shift they had to look past thousands of years of history emphasizing the privileged status of Israel as God's chosen people. To give up this special mantle in favor of a more inclusive perspective in which Gentiles would be welcomed must have been overwhelmingly difficult. The turning point comes in Acts 10—11, when Peter receives a challenging vision from the Holy Spirit regarding who should be granted entrance into God's kingdom. After Peter is confronted by his fellow Jews and explains what has happened, they all come to recognize the truth of what God is doing: "So then, even to the Gentiles God has granted repentance that leads to life" (Acts 11:18).

Paul further develops the concept of membership into God's kingdom in the book of Ephesians, where he eradicates the notion of "Jew" and "Gentile" and emphasizes the concept of oneness in Christ:

> For he himself is our peace, who has made the two one and has destroyed the barrier, the dividing wall of hostility, by abolishing in his flesh the law with its commands and regulations. . . .
>
> Consequently, you are no longer foreigners and aliens, but fellow citizens with God's people and also members of his household, built on the foundation of the apostles and prophets, with Christ Jesus himself as the chief cornerstone. (Eph 2:14-15, 19-20)

The English ministry of Open Door Presbyterian Church, a Korean immigrant church in Herndon, Virginia, used to have a more focused approach to its evangelistic efforts, given its ethnic and social identity. "Before, we were a yuppie, conservative, self-involved church," says pastor Dihan Lee. "But as we started to see people of different ethnicities come to faith in our service, we realized that this was where God was moving our church. We've since made a lot of progress in our evangelism."

Practice Relational, Long-Term Evangelism

Although Jesus did preach frequently to the masses, the bulk of his ministry was geared toward the few rather than the many. As Robert Coleman, professor emeritus of evangelism at Trinity International University, writes in *The Master Plan of Evangelism:*

[Jesus] concentrated Himself upon those who were to be the beginning of this leadership. Though He did what He could to help the multitudes, He had to devote Himself primarily to a few men, rather than the masses, in order that the masses could at last be saved. This was the genius of His strategy. . . .

Having called his men, Jesus made it a practice to be with them. This was the essence of his training program—just letting His disciples follow Him.[2]

Today's healthy Asian American churches are following a similar strategy: eschewing large evangelistic endeavors in favor of encouraging a more relational, one-on-one approach that more closely aligns with Asian cultural values. To reflect the similarity of this approach to Jesus' strategy during his earthly ministry, these churches call this *incarnational evangelism*.[3]

NewSong Church's Gibbons reflects on this concept of incarnational evangelism:

The best evangelism should be from people who know you as friends. Some of the best evangelism is done where people don't see faith as a lofty idea but where it's lived out in real world situations. So incarnational evangelism is about living in the culture, embracing the culture, knowing the culture, knowing the language and values of the culture.

Such an approach resonates more comfortably with many Asian American personalities because it is less about confrontation and more about building trust and connections over time. "We have had to be willing to reexamine the way we've traditionally viewed evangelism," says Ogimachi. "Evangelism isn't going to work due to a big marketing push; it is going to be through people who know people. It's very much a process that could take people months or years to come to Christ."

Today's healthy Asian American churches are thus not as focused on immediate conversions but on bringing each of their members and attendees to a closer relationship with Christ and with one another. It's not that the number of conversions is entirely irrelevant; however, today's approaches attempt to meld evangelism and discipleship to help people with their Christian walk over the course of their life. In his book *Pursuing the Pearl,* Fong writes about how his church has approached evangelism:

> When we state that our goal is to enable more unconvinced [Asian Americans] to become Christians, what we have in mind is far more expansive than leading them in the Sinner's Prayer and leaving it at that. Instead, we hope to initiate them into the lifelong pursuit of the pearl of great price. . . .
>
> Too many programs or approaches do not afford the unconvinced much dignity, because they do not allow them enough room to let a relationship with Christ emerge gradually and naturally.[4]

As a result, although some healthy Asian American churches have grown numerically at a fast pace, others have taken a more measured growth path. What is important for all these churches, however, is not primarily numbers but the depth and quality of relationships that are being formed, particularly between those within and outside of the church—similar to Jesus' approach in focusing on close relationships with a handful of people in order to reach the world. Greg Yee, director of leadership and congregational development for the Pacific Southwest Conference of the Evangelical Covenant Church, notes, "When I see a church doing well, it's highly invested in its community, either the one that surrounds them or the one they choose to get into. They are involved in the schools, the sports leagues, tutoring, everything. That's where I see a church's healthiness come out, when its people are invested in the neighborhood around them."

RELY ON THE HOLY SPIRIT

Due to a cultural tendency to place a high value on education and knowledge, Asian American churches can fall into the trap of relying too much on information about evangelism rather than relying on the Holy Spirit to be the leader and partner in the evangelistic process. Healthy Asian American churches understand that the work of evangelism is more God's work than their own, and they aim to rely on the Holy Spirit to guide their evangelistic efforts.

As is evident in the book of Acts, the main character in all the stories about conversion experiences is the Holy Spirit. For example, the first public evangelistic event in Scripture occurs in Acts 2, which recounts the arrival of the Holy Spirit on Pentecost. The Holy Spirit transforms the apostles into a group of tongue speakers, which serves to attract attention and draw a large crowd. Peter then takes advantage of the Spirit-created opportunity to share the gospel with those who were gathered around the disciples, resulting in an exponential evangelistic explosion: Acts 2:41 recounts that about three thousand new believers were added to the church that day alone. The disciples' main role is to pass along what they know and witnessed about Jesus. But it's the Holy Spirit who lays the groundwork for the conversion of souls, who cuts deep into the people's hearts and ultimately who brings people to faith.

Healthy Asian American churches rely on the Holy Spirit to lead their evangelistic efforts as opposed to relying on their own abilities and programs to win souls. New Song Church's Gibbons says, "Don't force evangelism. It is the Holy Spirit's initiative. Our evangelism does not have to be a cram-down-the-throat style. Asian Americans are not comfortable pushing an issue, and I think their approach can be more winsome."

As a result, Asian American Christians who desire to evangelize their friends and neighbors often do *not* explain their faith or the fact that they attend a church until well into the relationship, when trust has been established and an invitation to their church comes more naturally. They trust the Holy Spirit and keep their eyes and ears open for opportunities to build relationships with people that God has placed in their lives, and through the witness of their lives they demonstrate Christ without pushing tracts or spiritual laws at their neighbors.

In regard to relying on the Holy Spirit, one area where today's Asian

American churches need to grow is prayer. Asian American churches can learn a great deal from their immigrant and Asian counterparts, reclaiming the legacy of fervent prayer from generations past (such as in the early 1900s when a revival swept the fledgling Korean church and paved the way for its tremendous growth throughout the twentieth century). Even today, it's quite common to find early morning prayer meetings in full force at first-generation Asian churches, whereas the later generations have not yet demonstrated similar fervency. Who knows what the evangelistic impact would be if prayer became a main priority in today's Asian American congregations.

MEET FELT AS WELL AS SPIRITUAL NEEDS

Jesus did not just focus on people's souls. In fact, as he sent out his disciples for the first time, his instruction to them focused more on physical rather than spiritual healing: "Heal the sick, raise the dead, cleanse those who have leprosy, drive out demons" (Mt 10:8). There is no mention of forgiveness of sins, no encouragement to convince those who have been healed to believe in Jesus. Instead, in this phase of his ministry Jesus takes a long-term strategy, one in which he seeks to meet the felt needs of the people first in order to demonstrate his compassion and earn credibility. The healing of people's physical bodies and the cleansing of the public shame they derived from their illnesses was one of Jesus' method for softening their souls. In fact, Jesus often cautioned those he had healed not to tell others of his identity. He knew that there was a right time and place for people to be introduced to the truth of who he is.

Today, however, evangelism is often seen as a purely spiritual process. This process typically involves making a person aware of their distance from God, walking them through the rationale for Jesus' existence, and revealing how he bridges the spiritual gap between God and humans. Conversion is the goal. Although Jesus certainly had interactions with people with whom he had no history or long-term follow through (e.g., the Samaritan woman and Zacchaeus), he emphasized a more holistic approach, one that led with compassion for a person's immediate needs, leaving the discussions about spiritual realities for a future point. Although the evangelical church at large has done well at teaching Christians how to communicate the spiritual fate of unbelievers, today's healthy Asian American churches are finding ways to also recapture Jesus' long-term strategies.

For example, many healthy Asian American churches are discovering how significant healing ministries are for their congregation. Numerous Asian American church attendees have experienced significant dysfunction in their relationships or have been disillusioned by conflicts in their immigrant-church experience or have never been able to establish strong intimacy with God or others due to conflicts with their own parents. And although people today are not often in need of being healed of leprosy as in Jesus' time, there is a vast generation of Asian Americans who harbor psychological wounds and scars that need to be addressed, which may serve as a key evangelistic strategy in reaching unchurched and previously churched Asian Americans.

Greg Yee says that healing ministries have helped Asian American churches grow. "Once people hear that there is a church that provides this type of ministry, people start flocking," he says. "There is so much more addiction, trouble and brokenness out there, as well as people coming out of abusive situations or whose parents were abusive, than we may realize."

HOW HEALTHY ASIAN AMERICAN CHURCHES SHOW LEADERSHIP IN EVANGELISM

Given these biblical and theological principles, how are healthy Asian American churches demonstrating leadership in the area of evangelism? Although evangelism cannot be reduced to any particular model or strategy, there are seven notable ways in which healthy Asian American churches are evangelizing.

TAKE A MISSIOLOGICAL APPROACH

Before missionaries begin ministering in a foreign country, they typically undergo extensive preparations in order to engage the citizens of that unfamiliar context in an effective manner. They learn the language and cultural mores and ultimately immerse themselves among the people to whom they are hoping to evangelize. Leaders of healthy Asian American churches suggest that today's churches need to take the same approach in bringing the unchurched or previously churched to their congregations. For example, NewSong Church has identified a particular need its congregation has that may not exist in other congregations in the country. "On the West Coast, it's all about revealing your heart," Gibbons says. "In some other region of the U.S., the approach might be different."

On the opposite coast in Massachusetts, Cambridge Community Fellowship Church pastor Rah notes that though the demographics of his church is very similar to that of NewSong Church's, he must use a different approach. Within a mile or two of his church lie two of the most well-known names in higher education, Harvard University and Massachusetts Institute of Technology. Given that many of his congregants come from this educational context, Rah tailors his approach accordingly. "Using formulas and techniques geared toward the West Coast or Midwest won't work here," he says. "The academic questions that are raised here, and the pluralism here is more than you'll find in other parts of the country."

Healthy Asian American congregations know how important it is to thoroughly understand the culture and context of the audience they are trying to reach. Instead of merely imitating the latest evangelistic strategies that have had success with other types of churches and congregations, leaders of healthy Asian American churches know that they must be sensitive to the needs of their particular audience and adapt their approaches accordingly.

UNDERSTAND THE IMPACT OF POSTMODERNISM

Jesus certainly understood and displayed the principle of "knowing your audience." This allowed Jesus to tailor his messages to have maximum effect. Today's healthy Asian American churches need to similarly find ways to connect with their target audience. Though today's generation of Asian Americans has been significantly affected by its ethnic heritage and accompanying family dynamics, the influence of postmodernism is just as strong, and it needs to be considered in a church's evangelistic efforts.

In his recent book *Evangelism Outside the Box,* Rick Richardson outlines three new tenets of evangelism for today's postmodern age:[5]

- "Experience comes before explanation." Asian American pastors are incorporating this perspective by focusing less on providing logical explanations for why someone should believe and instead trying to show through their churches' community life that Christ is alive and well. "I think of Acts 2, the new community at Jerusalem, and how that was a contagious community," says Wayne Ogimachi. "We are trying to invite people into an environment where they can taste and see what new life in Christ is about. It's not just a rational, cognitive message. People often do need to experience before they can decide."

- "Belonging comes before believing." Richardson says that "evangelism is about helping people belong so that they can believe. Most people do not 'decide' to believe. In community, they 'discover' that they believe."[6] This is a tenet that rings true in Asian American churches. Unchurched Asian Americans connect to the church through various community activities and then, over time, realize that they have become attracted to Jesus and the Christian walk. Given the Asian American temperament to place a high value on community and relationships, the experience of belonging to a community of Christians often leads to an unbeliever placing their faith in Christ.

- "Images comes before word." Having been saturated with visual media since childhood, through television and movies in particular, Asian American seekers and nonbelievers respond to the use of images to communicate God's truth or to demonstrate sensitivity to the ethnic context of the congregation. This does not mean that the Word of God takes a second seat in church services of healthy Asian American congregations; it means that images are used when appropriate to help set the stage for the communication of biblical truths and values. Some of the healthy Asian American churches surveyed in this book, for example, employ movie clips or videos to enhance the worship experience. Others display works of classic or contemporary art. And still others pay specific attention to the atmosphere that is created in the sanctuary.[7] In these ways Asian American churches are going beyond merely a head-oriented communication of the Word to reach today's unchurched Asian Americans. They are striving to show creativity and innovation in the use of media, art and design to demonstrate that their churches understand the needs of this generation and ethnic audience.

FOCUS ON THE MARGINALIZED TO REACH THE MASSES

Although Asian American Christians have historically been less effective at serving the poor, the orphaned and the widowed—three groups of people who were priorities for Jesus while on earth—today's healthy Asian American churches are taking seriously Jesus' call to serve these underserved groups. "Our evangelism has to be focused on the least of the least, the marginalized," says Gibbons. "Who are the widows and orphans in your neighborhood? Your church has to be known for serving them."

Rah's Cambridge Community Fellowship Church, located in close proximity to lower-income residents, takes the same approach. He says:

> We try to do a lot of programs that are social justice or social action oriented. When we do things like a children's outreach in our neighborhood, even if we're not explicitly sharing the gospel, it's still evangelism. For this generation, evangelism is more about what you are doing on an individual, relational level. Our witness will be how we live our lives every day in our communities.

Rah's church is encouraging its members to live together in community, either near the church or in lower-income areas in Boston, and he hopes to see a trend in the church with more of its congregation choosing to live out the values of mercy and justice as a way to introduce the neighborhoods to Jesus (see chapter 9 for more on developing mercy and justice ministries).

Evergreen Baptist Church-LA is located in the city of Rosemead, a socio-economically and racially diverse community in southern California. In June 2004 the church organized an event called "The Rosemead Big Day," which entailed partnering with several other local Asian and multiethnic churches and coordinating thirty-five community projects for members of these participating congregations. A quadrilingual pamphlet (in Chinese, Vietnamese, Spanish and English) was also prepared with information about the churches involved. Executive pastor Jonathan Wu says, "Our people washed cars, removed yard and trash debris, cleaned alleys and public streets, visited convalescent centers, painted walls, trimmed trees, and took care of simple home repairs. Everywhere we heard the echoes, 'Thank you for your kindness,' or 'I didn't know that churches would do this on a Sunday.' " Wu hopes that by being visible in the community, new opportunities for outreach and relationship building will occur.

Yet one challenge for Evergreen Baptist Church-LA, which often also confronts other Asian American churches, is how to be missional within a community when the church often draws its congregation from a larger metropolitan area. "Our congregation is highly educated and professional. Will someone from the Rosemead neighborhood, someone who's not college-educated or who just came from overseas, feel like a stranger in our congregation? What are ways we can be incarnational when we don't live in our church's neighborhood?" asks Wu. Although some, like Nicole Gon, are choosing to live in the Rosemead community, Wu believes that about 95 percent of Evergreen's attendees do not.

This continues to be a growing area for healthy Asian American churches. Even if visible and significant progress has not been made in terms of seeing its local community change, the vision and priorities to do so are visible and known in these churches. "We must focus on the marginalized," says Gibbons. "That's how we'll reach the masses."

PURSUE RIGHT RELATIONSHIPS

A fourth way that successful Asian American churches are demonstrating their leadership in evangelism is by placing a high priority on authentic and healthy relationships. Given that Asian Americans value community, one might assume that their relationships are strong and thriving. However, other cultural values such as "saving face" hinder them from developing deep, honest relationships, and the Asian American churches that recognize this do what they can to challenge those cultural problems.

Grace Community Covenant Church's Wong says, "The irony is that relationships are so important to Asian Americans, but we're so inept at building them because we're not used to being real. We should present ourselves, with all our flaws, to each other and to God because that's where the healing comes. But the shame aspect of Asian culture is a hindrance."

In particular, Wong notes that the area of emotional health is a challenging one for Asian Americans. "If people are prone to depression or struggle with feeling unhappy, they have a hard time acknowledging that. So as someone who finds myself in depressive thought cycles all the time, I am willing to talk about it, so that others can be willing to talk about it."

In fact, one key factor that appears to help Asian American churches live more openly and honestly before one another is having leaders who self-disclose. Particularly for an Asian American audience, whose tendency to save face inclines people not to share their struggles, having pastoral leaders who are willing to publicly disclose their struggles sets an example for how to be transparent with one another. "One of my pastors recently shared during a sermon that he has been feeling spiritually bankrupt and has been struggling. I think it was his most powerful sermon in the last ten years," says Ken Fong. "The more I explore the Scriptures, the more I visit the cross of Jesus. If you come to me as another messy, smelly Christian looking for help and guidance, I know how to point you to that cross because I have been there myself."

At NewSong Church, Gibbons and his fellow leaders similarly model a relational style that encourages vulnerability. He says, "We try to encourage personal confession both in the pulpit and the private arena. We want the norm in our church to be acknowledging and admitting that we're screwed up. That's why one of the slogans we use for our church is that we're a church for the misfits." The evangelistic benefit of being such a church is clear: the more that people understand that they will not be judged for who they are, but accepted as they are, the more likely it is that they will stay with the church long enough to understand the gospel message.

PRESENT A POWERFUL AND RELEVANT WORSHIP EXPERIENCE

Another way that healthy Asian American churches demonstrate evangelism leadership is by creating worship experiences that are powerful and relevant. In particular, sermons tend to be of key importance. Lighthouse Christian Church's Ogimachi says, "We try to deal with tough topics that would be interesting and helpful to an unbeliever as well as a believer. Any topic we deal with, we want an unbeliever to say, 'That sounds interesting.' We only get to address people's real need—to repent of their sins and receive salvation—when we come through the door of their felt needs." In Ogimachi's sermons, he strives to answer felt-need questions such as, How do you make relationships work, and how do you heal from damaged relationships? What makes life significant? How do you make marriage work?

Similarly, at NewSong Church, the pastors strive to make both sermons and sermon titles current and appealing. One recent sermon series titled "Taboo" addressed hot-potato issues such as homosexuality, hell and money. "The sermons communicate a value that this is a church that talks about topics in the Bible that are hard to understand or that other churches won't talk about," says former associate pastor Nancy Sugikawa. "It helps our congregation know that this church is dealing with real life issues."

In addition to focusing on the sermon, healthy Asian American churches also put a great deal of thought into how their worship service is perceived by visitors and unchurched Asian Americans. For better or for worse, Asian Americans are influenced by first impressions, so strong churches aim to capitalize on that mindset by offering quality wherever they can.

For Ogimachi, a church's worship service is both a critical evangelism tool and a barometer for the church's self-image. "I view the worship service as the heart of the church. If the heart is healthy, it can pump blood and life into the other parts of the body," he says. "And if people feel good about their worship service, they feel good about their church." As a result, Ogimachi aims for a service that reflects quality and excellence. For example, Lighthouse Christian Church has held auditions for those who are interested in participating in the worship-team ministry, and it invests in training the worship-team members to keep the quality high.

Ogimachi is vigilant about not using terminology or language that might not be understood by an unchurched visitor. Having come from a non-Christian family, he always asks himself, *Would this make sense to my brother, or would my parents want to hear a message like this?* Gibbons takes a similar approach at NewSong Church, where he thinks specifically about the language used during a Sunday service. "We try to be ruthless with religious jargon," he says. "We don't use religious language, but we use language that everyone can understand and use to grow spiritually. In our congregation, we have people with theological training from the best of seminaries sitting next to an agnostic, and both should get something out of our service."

EMBRACE THE POSSIBILITY OF DIVERSITY

Each of the churches that were part of this book's survey differs in terms of how it identifies itself and its target audience from an ethnic perspective. Some are explicitly geared for Asian Americans; others are implicitly designed that way; and still others aim for a more multiethnic focus even though the demographics lean predominantly Asian American. But regardless of where the church sits on the spectrum of possibilities, in all of these churches the leaders acknowledge that sensitivity to other ethnicities is crucial and can contribute to evangelistic progress. In even explicitly identified Asian American churches, many different ethnicities can be represented, and often non-Asians will find themselves drawn to these congregations despite the ethnic focus.

"Our initial focus was to reach second- and third-generation Asian Americans and their friends," says Grace Community Covenant Church's Wong. "Once we started realizing that vision, I saw that 'and their friends' meant becoming more multiethnic." Wong has continued to stay the course in terms of focusing on Asian Americans, but he continues "to preach on the need to reach across cultural and class lines as an expression of social justice and the prophetic voice of the church."

At Evergreen Baptist Church-LA, which is predominantly Asian American (though the pastoral staff seeks to become more multiethnic), the potential witness that a healthy multiethnic community can demonstrate is a clear reason to pursue it. But the pastoral leaders acknowledge that being open to others different from oneself can be risky business. In his book *Secure in God's Embrace,* Fong writes:

> Coming together as diverse fellow adoptees of God is truly wonderful and rare. Simply being together as a community in Christ can be a foretaste of heaven itself. But there is still so much to learn, so much blindness to uncover. As one of my Latin American Christian brothers once wrote to me, "In a truly multiethnic [gathering], no one is comfortable."[8]

No matter what the ethnic composition or target is of today's Asian American churches, they need to accept that they are already multiethnic communities because most are usually comprised of more than one ethnic group. Thus they need be open to change that comes from the natural metamorphosis of the congregation as members invite others who may not fit the church's target demographic. They need to determine how best to serve both their target audience as well as their future multiethnicity. They also need to embrace the evangelistic benefits that come from having a variety of cultures under one roof.

DON'T ABANDON TRADITIONAL APPROACHES

Despite the emphasis that many of today's healthy Asian American churches are placing on new evangelistic approaches, they also acknowledge that there is still immense value in traditional ways of doing evangelism. For some seekers the immediacy and power of an altar call may be the best means for the Holy Spirit to take initiative in their lives, and so some churches have made a point to continue the practice while concurrently engaging in alternative methods.

For example, at the English ministry of Open Door Presbyterian Church altar calls are given when "there is a clear point of contact with seekers in the message," says pastor Lee.

> Generally, the way our invitations go, at the end of the message, we ask people to raise their hands while their heads are bowed. And after hands have been raised, we pray for them and then encourage them to seek out one of the pastors, or talk to a friend they came with. Generally we get one to two hands to receive Christ and a good number of people who would like to recommit their lives or commit to a certain application.

Grace May, former pastor of Chinese Christian Church of New England (Brookline, Mass.), found that altar calls had a good response in her largely immigrant congregation, particularly among the younger generation. "At CCCNE, an altar call offers a sister or a brother an opportunity to respond to the message or the stirring of the Spirit. It is a poignant moment in the worship service, where a person enjoys intimate communion with God, witnessed by another member of the family," May says. Ultimately, the decision to focus on newer models or stick with older models, or do both, comes down to understanding one's particular congregation and knowing what will work best to reach them.

So while today's healthy Asian American churches are not overly concerned about numbers when it comes to evangelism, at the same time they take the Great Commission seriously. At a recent Sunday service at NewSong Church, the baptism of numerous new believers was clearly a time of celebration and joy for all those in attendance, with raucous cheers and whistles greeting each newly baptized person as he or she was introduced to the congregation.

No one method or model will fit a church, and, in fact, evangelism is ultimately less about strategies and programs, and much more about the heart of the people in the church. How much have they embraced God's own heart for the lost? Do they care less about serving those within the church and more about reaching those outside its walls? Are all of the church's programs geared not just to strengthen those within the body but to grow the body itself? Ultimately, strong Asian American churches recognize the biblical truth that "it is not the healthy who need a doctor, but the sick" (Lk 5:31).

SLOW AND STEADY PROGRESS

Rick Richardson notes that true progress in evangelism is not for the uncommitted. "It takes a disproportionate commitment for evangelism to reach the level of intensity of other values and priorities. What will it take for you and your church?"[9]

For today's healthy Asian American churches, the road to effective evangelism is not merely measured by yearly conversions. Progress is more difficult to ascertain due to changing attitudes and strategies that focus more on the process and journey of coming to Christ than on a singular moment of decision to accept Christ. And while not every church in this survey has taken the same approach to evangelism, the consensus seems to favor community-oriented, one-on-one relationship development—a far different strategy than the age of large evangelistic rallies and crusades—which resonates well with the cultural background of these Asian American, postmodern congregations. As they encourage their church members to enter into relationships with those whom God has placed in their path, and as these churches' leaders demonstrate what it means to live openly and honestly before God and with one another, healthy Asian American congregations are slowly and steadily reaching more unchurched or previously churched Asian Americans. It may take a lifetime to win a soul for Christ, but healthy Asian American churches know that the reward will be an eternity to enjoy the victory.

7

MULTIGENERATIONAL HOUSEHOLDS

PETER CHA, PAUL KIM AND DIHAN LEE

"How very good and pleasant it is when
God's people live together in unity!"
PS 133:1

DANIEL WAS SITTING ALONE IN THE EMPTY SANCTUARY, reflecting and praying. Particularly on this day, the first day of his ministry, the young pastor was deeply thankful for the many blessings he had recently received: the successful completion of his seminary education, the gift of his new marriage and now an opportunity to serve in a growing Korean immigrant church. After offering a prayer of thanksgiving, Daniel made his way toward the senior pastor's office, feeling excited and nervous at the same time. He felt very privileged to begin his ministry journey under a seasoned pastor. At the same time, Daniel was uncertain about many aspects of his future ministry at this church, largely because he knew very little about the senior pastor under whom he would serve. Before he knocked on the pastor's door, the second-generation pastor paused for a moment, gathering his thoughts and rehearsing greetings in Korean.

Reverend Oh warmly invited Daniel into his office. The pastor's welcome, however, was a brief one as he immediately began to express his expectations for Daniel. The senior pastor did not present a long list of responsibilities and duties. Instead, Rev. Oh succinctly but unequivocally stated, "Your only job at this church is to follow my directions and to train your young leaders to obey their elders." Surprised and jolted, the young pastor simply stood there speechless, not sure how he should respond.

When Daniel sat down in his new office, he couldn't help but continually think about his short interaction with the senior pastor. When Daniel accepted the invitation to come and serve as the pastor of the English-speaking congregation of this immigrant church, he and his wife were filled with many dreams and visions for this young congregation. Having grown up in immigrant churches, they were quite aware of some of the major challenges second-generation ministries face and of the many changes these churches needed to embrace if they were to effectively reach out to Americanized younger generations. Hence, Daniel and his wife were eager to try out a number of innovative ministry strategies and tools they acquired from their college campus-ministry experiences, seminary education and the great internship experience they had in a predominantly Caucasian congregation.

After his brief exchange with the senior pastor, however, Daniel was not sure whether he would be allowed to provide such leadership to this congregation. After taking a deep breath, he folded his hands on the desk and began to pray. And this time, Daniel offered a prayer of earnest petition, seeking God's strength and mercy for him and his new ministry.

THE CHALLENGE OF INTERGENERATIONAL CONFLICTS IN THE CHURCH

Unfortunately, the experience and the challenges that young pastor Daniel encountered are often repeated in hundreds of other Asian immigrant congregations in North America. To be sure, generational conflict is becoming more visible also in the wider Christian community. Recent studies indicate that a growing number of Caucasian churches in North America are engaged in various forms of intergenerational struggles, resulting in "worship wars" and in the formation of generation-specific congregations. Nevertheless, some of the unique aspects of Asian American cultures and of immigrant life dynamics make generational conflict within Asian immigrant churches particularly complex and challenging.

Given that the majority of Asian immigrants came to the United States after the Immigration Act of 1965, the first wave of second-generation young people has entered their adulthood. They are no longer malleable and silent in their families and in their communities. Influenced by American culture and its social values, these young adults are asserting their opinions, claiming their rights and even challenging their elders' traditional value systems and perspectives. Many immigrant parents and community leaders, meanwhile, are hurt and alarmed by their young people's actions, causing some to react by digging deeper into their traditional mode of thinking and practice. As a result, the generational and cultural gulf between the two generations widens while the tension escalates.

In many ways Confucian-based Asian cultures both strengthen and undermine the intergenerational ties in Asian American settings. This is particularly true in familial settings. On the one hand, their strong emphases on filial piety and on the primacy of family encourage both generations to fortify and value their intergenerational family ties, particularly the parent-child relationship. On the other hand, however, their unswerving support for hierarchical relational order promotes intergenerational ties that emphasize the obedience and submission of the younger, an aspect that alienates many second-generation young people. Consequently, while both parties might value the importance of intergenerational ties, they nonetheless disagree on what these ties should look like.

Many frustrated and embattled Asian immigrants and their children thus turn to their ethnic churches for guidance and direction. However, many immigrant congregations are unable to respond to this challenge effectively since they are also embroiled in similar intergenerational conflicts. In many ways the relationship between the two generations is even more volatile and contentious in these churches. A pastor summed up the hardships second-generation members and leaders face in the following way:

> Cultural and language barriers that exist between first and second-generation Koreans work against their [second-generation members'] assuming wider roles in the church. . . . Rarely will their gifts be utilized in making important decisions for the church. Even though some of them . . . have important professional positions in the workplace, in the eyes of the first-generation leadership, they are still children. . . . Therefore, any pastor or church leader interested in keeping second-generation Koreans in the immigrant church must face the hard fact: There is not enough incentive for them to stay in a church that is dominated by the Korean-speaking members.[1]

Discouraged by their current experiences and bleak future, frustrated second-generation leaders and members have been deserting their immigrant churches in large numbers. Although it is difficult to ascertain an exact number, some of the surveys done during the 1990s, for instance, indicated that between 80 and 90 percent of second-generation Korean American and more than 70 percent of Chinese American young adults leave their immigrant churches after college. Some of those who joined this "Silent Exodus" organize their own independent congregations while others attend predominantly-Anglo congregations. The rest, tragically, drop out of the church scene all together, drifting away from the Christian faith.

Given this context, developing healthy intergenerational ties is a critical task for Asian congregations in North America. For these churches the task of developing wholesome intergenerational partnerships is, among other things, a matter of long-term survival as it affects their ability to retain their American-born young people. Furthermore, given that many Asian immigrant families significantly wrestle with various forms of intergenerational conflict, these churches' successful growth in this area can uniquely position them to provide invaluable services to their members, serving as places of healing and reconciliation. In short, the wellness and survival of most Asian immigrant churches are greatly dependent on their ability to form healthy intergenerational ties, and their ability to relate to and partner with emerging generations of American-born young people. This chapter will probe and explore various aspects of this critical project.

CHURCH AS A HOUSEHOLD OF GOD

Because of the critical and challenging nature of this project, it is imperative that the growth in this area of congregational life is fully informed and guided by appropriate biblical principles and sound theological reflection. In the epistle to the Ephesians, the apostle Paul presents the church as God's masterpiece. As he explains why the church is the chosen entity through which God's "manifold wisdom" and glory are to be fully revealed, Paul highlights the unity of the church as one of its defining, majestic characteristics that brings glory to our God. As a way of illustrating this powerful truth, Paul, in Ephesians 2, directly addresses one of the deepest sociocultural divisions that plagued the early church: the tension-filled relationship between Jewish Christians and their Gentile counterparts. In this oft-quoted passage Paul doesn't call Christians to work out their differences in order to achieve Christian unity. Instead, he simply reminds them that Christ has already achieved their unity, that he broke down the dividing wall of hostility when he died on the cross. In light of what the Savior has already accomplished, Paul then calls Christians to appropriate this new reality, to enjoy a life of reconciliation and unity with all God's people.

To yet further emphasize this achieved reality of reconciliation and unity among God's people, Paul then ends the passage by using a powerful metaphor to describe what the church is: he calls it "God's household." In Ephesians 2:19 he writes, "Consequently, you are no longer foreigners and strangers, but fellow citizens with God's people and also members of his household." Paul intentionally chooses a metaphor that is particularly meaningful and potent in first-century Mediterranean culture, a metaphor that would elicit from his readers sentiments of loyalty, love and commitment. Paul aims to communicate that the church is not another social organization or voluntary association with which individuals can casually choose to affiliate or disaffiliate.

So what does it mean to view and understand the church as a household of God? What are some of the implications of this truth? To begin with, when a person becomes a Christian, he or she joins a family, a covenant family of God's people. With our new birth comes a new family. With our new spiritual identity comes a new social identity. And unlike friendships, we don't get to choose our family members; we are simply born into existing relationships. There is a firm sense of "givenness" about family relationships; you cannot disown your family members or walk away from them even when things get tough.

Furthermore, the metaphor of a household strongly emphasizes the multigenerational aspect of the community of God's people; it doesn't consist of one cohort group of similar ages. It assumes the presence of spiritual grandparents, uncles, aunts, parents, cousins and siblings. The term *household* (*oikos*) in the New Testament refers to the wider circle of an extended family, not the modern nuclear family. It is in such a setting that the older members are to be wise role models for the younger ones, and the younger members in turn are to pay respect to the elders while raising their own children in love (Tit 2:1-8).

How does today's Asian American congregation develop its identity as a household of God? How does a congregation function as a healthy family of God's people? Particularly, how should a congregation express unity and oneness among different generations when the cultural barriers so easily divide them? This is especially challenging in our world where churches are often perceived as a spiritual supermarket, a place where individualistic and consumeristic desires are satisfied.

In the rest of this chapter we will explore various ways in which Asian American congregations can intentionally work on bridging the generational divide by learning to function as a healthy household of God. In doing so, since ethnic immigrant churches make up the vast majority of the Asian American Christian community (currently, Korean immigrant churches alone number 4,000) and since intergenerational conflicts are particularly pronounced in these crosscultural settings, we will primarily focus on the experience of one Asian immigrant church that has been going through a rich journey in this particular area.

BRINGING GENERATIONS TOGETHER: AN ASIAN IMMIGRANT CONGREGATION'S EXPERIENCES

A number of studies have found that second-generation ministries in most Asian immigrant churches go through certain stages as they grow in size and develop in maturity. In the beginning stages, ministry for second-generation young adults is fully supported and supervised by the first-generation congregation; the former is very dependent on the latter. Then, as it grows, the second-generation ministry begins to form its own identity and ministry vision, gradually moving toward financial and organizational independence from its "mother" church. Once it achieves a degree of autonomy, the second-generation ministry often chooses to become an independent church, leaving behind the immigrant church to start up another second-generation-oriented ministry to provide spiritual care for the next cohort group of second-generation young adults.

This cycle is repeated in many immigrant church contexts, partly because healthy, long-term intergenerational ties are not successfully pursued and nurtured. To put it differently, second-generation ministry groups seek complete independence largely because they perceive that first-generation congregations desire control and domination. First-generation congregations, on the other hand, often send out the second-generation congregations with a sense of relief because they are worn out by the conflict-ridden and contentious nature of multigenerational community life. In short, both parties decide to go separate ways partly because they conclude that the goal of achieving healthy intergenerational ties is too costly and too daunting.

To be sure, the project of becoming a healthy multigenerational "household of God" can be costly; it requires long-term commitment, sacrifice and concerted efforts from both first- and second-generation congregations.

However, believing that the development of such a partnership can richly reward both sides and that such an expression of unity will honor God, a number of Asian immigrant churches have been making intentional efforts to grow in this critical area. Open Door Presbyterian Church, a twenty-year old Korean immigrant church in northern Virginia, is one of them.

About ten years ago the second-generation young people of Open Door Presbyterian Church formed their own English-speaking congregation and began to move toward organizational autonomy. However, during the past four years the leadership of the first- and second-generation congregations took specific steps to reverse this movement, consciously making efforts to bring the two generations closer together. What prompted this church to redirect its orientation on intergenerational relationship? What are some specific steps this church has taken that allowed it to overcome many obstacles on the way?

BUILDING A UNIFIED PASTORAL TEAM

In order to develop a congregation that enjoys healthy intergenerational relationships, it is foundational that the pastoral team models this first. Like other immigrant churches that serve multiple language groups, this church also has multiple full-time pastoral staff members serving these groups: three pastors, including the senior pastor, serve the Korean-speaking congregation and four pastors lead the English-speaking congregation and the youth group. These pastoral staff members come from the same ethnic background, sharing some aspects of common ethnic and cultural heritage. Yet, given the presence of language and generational barriers (one pastor is first-generation, two are 1.5-generation while the rest are second-generation) within this team, the possibility of crosscultural conflict and miscommunication is always present. Furthermore, because some of these pastors have experienced many negative aspects of intergenerational relationships in their previous immigrant churches, feelings of distrust and suspicion can easily resurface. So how does this particular team overcome these and other obstacles and become strongly united across cultural and generational divides?

Building a healthy pastoral team begins with a set of regular practices that develop strong relationships among the pastors; it begins with a set of informal activities that increase "relational capital" among the team members. In addition to their weekly pastoral staff meetings, where they openly discuss various ministry-related issues and pray for one another, the pastors regularly eat lunch together, taking turns providing the meal for the whole team, sharing food as well as their life concerns. Beyond these fellowship meals, the pastors have also found other ways to strengthen their relationships, whether it is by playing Ping-Pong after lunch or by going on day-long fishing trips together. Serving in a rapidly growing church where their combined membership doubled to more than one thousand people during the past three years, each pastor of Open Door Presbyterian Church carries a heavy workload. However, they see these team-building activities as an essential part of their ministry in this immigrant church because it enables them to strengthen their relational and ministerial ties. The fact that many of these pastors, whose ages range from the mid-twenties to late-forties, have been serving together for several years and that they are willing to make a long-term commitment to their shared ministry and to one another bears wonderful testimony to their intergenerational and intercultural friendship and partnership.

STRENGTHENING RELATIONAL TIES AMONG THE MULTIGENERATIONAL MEMBERS

Building healthy intergenerational ties within the immigrant church may begin with the pastoral team, but it can't end there. In order for a multigenerational immigrant congregation to function as a healthy household of God, intentional relationship building needs to occur between the first- and second-generation congregation members as well. Recognizing the critical importance of this, Open Door Presbyterian Church has intentionally created time and space where members from both congregations can come together regularly and deepen their fellowship ties. Each year, both congregations participate in a joint Easter sunrise service, expressing their unity through their bilingual worship service. During this annual joint service, one of the English-speaking pastors preaches while the senior pastor translates the sermon into Korean. Twice each year, they come together to celebrate baptism services, welcoming new members into their multigenerational, bicultural church family. Finally, whenever either congregation is ordaining pastors or lay leaders (elders and deacons), the entire church comes together to mark the occasion. Although bilingual services can sometimes be a tedious exercise, by choosing to celebrate these important events together, members of the two congregations experience and reinforce their oneness in Christ.

These two congregations also share some fellowship activities. Each year, they participate in a church-wide picnic, where the members from both congregations can meet one another and mingle with others as they play a variety of "ice breaker" outdoor games. They also come together for church-wide banquets on various occasions, including Easter, Thanksgiving and Christmas. It has become a tradition that the second-generation congregation cooks for Thanksgiving. This past year the young people prepared thirty-six super-size turkeys to feed over a thousand people. Donning gloves to serve turkey dinners to the older members of the Korean-speaking congregation, in the midst of laughter, talking and the sharing of a big meal the picture that emerges is that of a household of God.

TOWARD AN INTERDEPENDENT MODEL OF MINISTRY

While strengthening relationships between members from different generations is invaluable, healthy intergenerational ties within congregations need to be accompanied also by intentional intergenerational partnership in ministry. In many ways, Open Door Presbyterian Church's Korean-speaking and English-speaking congregations are still autonomous entities. Each congregation is led by its own pastoral staff and elected lay leaders. Each congregation also has its own operating budget, managing its own day to day functions. During the past three years, however, the church leadership has moved toward developing what they call an interdependent model of ministry, a model in which both congregations remain autonomous and yet choose to *serve* one another and *serve with* one another in their shared mission.

Last year, as an expression of their desire to increase this sense of shared ministry, the pastors of both congregations jointly drafted new statements that articulate their shared vision, mission, faith convictions and core values. After receiving input and approval by their respective lay leaders, the pastors began to articulate their new shared vision, core values and the philosophy of ministry to their own members. In doing so, the pastors wanted to emphasize unity in their *being* as well as *doing*, in who they *are* as well as who they are *becoming*.

How do these shared vision and values of ministry get expressed in the life of the church? How do they become more than a mere statement on a sheet of paper? In short, they must be practiced. They must be embodied in the life of the church so that these values can be internalized by each member and can become integral parts of the congregational culture. For instance, one of the newly formulated core values reads, "We believe in church as a hospital, where broken people can come as they are and find refuge and healing (Matthew 11:28-30)." Given that traditional Asian culture tends to discourage individuals and families from wrestling with their pain and hurt in a public setting, this church decided to adopt this particular value as a key value. In implementing this value that is now shared by both congregations, they have found ways to work together in bringing healing to hurting members in their congregations.

One autumn Sunday morning, the second-generation congregation of the Open Door Presbyterian Church was holding a special worship service to launch an exciting new ministry called *klēma*, which in Greek means "branch." The ministry, spearheaded by some of the second-generation members and fully supported by pastors from both congregations, aims to serve a number of individuals with various disabilities in the church. Too often Asian churches ignore disabled individuals, viewing them as burdens that their families need to bear. Compounding the problem is a pervasive cultural perspective in Asian settings that tend to view disabled children as a family shame. Many parents don't bring their disabled children to their churches due to this shame factor and because many immigrant churches offer no special resources for these children. Given this context, the launching of the *klēma* ministry is even more meaningful and inspirational to this young congregation. (They named this ministry *klēma* to highlight that those with disabilities who are often neglected and shunted aside are actually honored and precious parts of the church body.)

This new ministry is even more meaningful to the Open Door Presbyterian Church household because from the beginning it has brought together Korean-speaking and English-speaking congregations. The idea of this ministry was formed when a group of second-generation members noticed that several families that attend the Korean-speaking congregation have children with various disabilities. Noticing that these children's special needs were not being met by the church, these young professionals, many of whom work with disabled children in the public school system, proposed the ministry plan to the pastoral team. Their proposal was enthusiastically received, not only by the pastoral staff team but also by the Korean-speaking congregation.

As soon as the ministry was set in motion, the church leadership secured the necessary funds to build ramps, to create a specialized room and to provide needed educational materials and special equipment. A growing number of families began to enroll their children with special needs in this new program, and many parents volunteered their time to make sure that the program would have a strong start. Even high school students whose siblings were in the program stepped forward to help out. The launching of this new ministry, in short, brought together members from all different age groups.

On the Sunday morning when the congregation gathered to commission this new ministry, they were celebrating the beginning of a much-needed ministry. At the same time, this young congregation was also celebrating a very concrete form of partnership it was beginning with its Korean-speaking congregation. But this time it was entering into this partnership primarily as a leader and a provider, a relatively new role for this young congregation.

The launching of the *klēma* ministry is one of many examples of how the first- and second-generation congregations intentionally reinforce their ministry partnership, building an interdependent model of ministry.

INTERGENERATIONAL PARTNERSHIP IN MISSION

In addition to enriching the life of a given congregation, a strong intergenerational partnership can also enhance the effectiveness of a church's ministry of outreach, locally and globally. Recognizing that members of the Korean-speaking and the English-speaking congregations bring different sets of gifts, training and resources, Open Door Presbyterian Church intentionally uses their summer mission projects to further promote their intergenerational partnership. While these joint events might require additional effort and preparation, they found that the rewards and benefits far outweigh the costs involved.

It has been another long, hot summer day in the Gambian village. They have been treating patients all day, and yet there is still a long line of people, patiently waiting to receive medical attention. This is the site of a mobile medical clinic, operated by a team of short-term missionaries from the Open Door congregations. The team, ranging in age from twenty-two to sixty, consists of members from the Korean-speaking and the English-speaking congregations. John and Sam, both second-generation young adults, along with Mr. Park and Mr. Kim, older first-generation Koreans, are trying to guide and organize, with varied success, the steady stream of people. David and Peter, both second-generation medical students issue medicine at the pharmacy table while Dr. Lee and Dr. Shin, both first-generation medical doctors, along with several first-generation nurses work the various care tables—including those for pediatrics, obstetrics, skin care and eye care. Of course, this is no modern hospital—just some makeshift tables, a truckload of donated medicine, and a group of multigenerational Korean American Christians from one church.

Before the mission trip began, no one was quite sure how the experience in Gambia would turn out. There was a level of concern shared by both first-

and second-generation team members since nothing like this had been done before at the church. This was the largest interdependent ministry effort this church had attempted. The building of partnership began even before the team hit Gambian soil. Fundraising was done jointly. Training was done together in both languages.

Elder Lee, the first-generation leader of the entire team set a huge precedent when he declared that there would be no distinction by age or generation. To make this egalitarian ethos concrete, he had everyone, including first-generation elders and deacons go by their English first name. If they did not have one, they made one up. It was a strange experience, to say the least, to have a second-generation young person calling an elder by his first name. In essence, under Elder Lee's leadership, this short-term missions team created a new culture for itself. It made a big difference.

On the Sunday when the entire church gathered to send them off, it was clear that they were sending off a unified team. Furthermore, the two sponsoring congregations also experienced a strengthened unity as they gathered to pray for this missions team. Sons prayed for their fathers who were going; fathers prayed for their daughters who were going. The entire church was invested in the team.

After they reached their mission field, the team continued building strong bonds crossing generational boundaries. Each day began with team worship, done in a mixture of Korean and English. Each day, the team would work the stations, using interpreters, until late afternoon. As they worked with a steady stream of sick Gambians, their generation and cultural differences were muted by the urgent needs and the nature of the ministry. "Can you wrap a bandage?" "Would you take him to the eye-care station?" These were the questions that mattered on site. As they worked side by side for two weeks, they learned to communicate with one another verbally and nonverbally. The language barrier that seemed so insurmountable at church seemed almost nonexistent.

There were also lighter moments that contributed to the building of intimate relationships. The men agreed not to shave the entire time they were in Gambia. Elder and young, all sporting beards, competing for the darkest shade. After dinner, young second-generation men sitting next to their elders on a rug, asked the older men about dating and how to find a wife. Much laughter ensued into the night. Just guys being guys. No cultural barrier there.

When the two-week-long ministry was coming to a close, the team retreated to a beach on the western shore of Gambia and took time to debrief and share their experiences. What took place was an amazing work of reconciliation. Several second-generation people shared about how this trip was a healing experience for them. Wounds and bitterness they had harbored against the first-generation immigrants disappeared as they were able to see their elders as men and women who love the Lord. Likewise, the first-generation team members learned how to respect and appreciate the gifts of their younger brothers and sisters. One second-generation member observed that had they gone on a short-term mission with their peer group alone, they would have returned with their team members as good friends, but with this trip they are returning to the United States as a strong family, with spiritual uncles, aunts, brothers and sisters.

Since they have returned, the intergenerational ties forged in the mission field continue to bring team members together. It is not uncommon to find former team members from the two congregations hugging each other in the church hallways and catching up with one another. Bonds have formed between the generations that cut through cultural, language and generational boundaries. Given this and other benefits, Open Door Presbyterian Church continues to send multigenerational mission teams to Gambia and Uzbekistan every summer.

EMBARKING ON THE JOURNEY

As with any household, there are seasons of growth and seasons of setbacks. What you have seen from these examples is Open Door Presbyterian Church in its best moments. The pastors of the church are the first to confess that there have been many challenging moments as well. One particular issue that they continue to wrestle with is trust. The pastors realize that interdependency within a Korean American setting usually begins with a trust deficit. Many from the English-speaking generation in particular come to the church having already learned to distrust the Korean-speaking generation—largely because of their own family and past church experiences. Everyone is learning that the journey toward interdependency takes the church through a history of pain, scars and distrust. This is by no means easy. The inertia of established patterns of behavior and thinking ensures that interdependency is not a quick fix or even an easy solution; it is one that must be forged very intentionally, with much wisdom, creativity and prayer.

Getting to this point in Open Door Presbyterian Church's journey took ten years, and the pastors see this as just the beginning. The journey might seem daunting, but being a household is a core value of this church—one that both congregations have covenanted to—and the church has gone far enough on this journey to know that the body of Christ is more richly and powerfully expressed and experienced when there is mutuality and love among the Korean- and English-speaking congregations. That is why Open Door Presbyterian Church is committed to this journey to genuine interdependency even though it has taken them and will continue to take them into difficult and often uncharted places.

There is a growing number of Asian immigrant churches that are also recognizing the significance of this aspect of congregational life and are intentionally building strong intergenerational ties and partnerships; thankfully, Open Door Presbyterian Church is not a rarity. These churches have embarked on an important journey, a journey of becoming healthy households of God.

Perhaps you are a pastor or a member of an Asian immigrant church who is very discouraged and frustrated by deep generational and cultural divides in your church. If so, perhaps God is calling you and your church to begin this journey that can, through his grace, transform you and your church. But how do you begin such a journey? What are some specific steps you should take? What lessons can we learn from Open Door Presbyterian Church's experiences?

Pray. At the beginning of his epistle to Ephesians, the apostle Paul reminds his readers that he is praying ceaselessly for their church, their "household of God" (Eph 1:15-23). Like other Korean churches, Open Door Presbyterian Church is a praying church. It has a daily early morning prayer service and weekly late-night prayer meetings. Becoming a God-honoring church is a process of corporate sanctification, a process that cannot be done without the power and the work of the Holy Spirit. Are you praying for your church with persistence as Paul had done?

Listen. A wise Christian leader once said that unity should not be a goal for Christians but a reward we receive when we learn to listen to the voice of the same Lord. As we wrestle with various crosscultural and intergenerational challenges in our congregations, do we pause and listen to his voice together? Do we practice the headship of Christ in our churches?

Know who you are. Although our culture tells us that the church is like a spiritual supermarket, where potential customers can come and sample goods as individuals, the Bible tells us that the church is household of God, a family in which Christians strengthen their ties to their heavenly Father as well as to their brothers and sisters in Christ. Which image of the church does your church embrace? Which do you embrace?

Spend time together. Members of a healthy family spend time with one another, sharing their joys and concerns and deepening their commitment to one another. In our churches, people from different generations usually do not mingle; often the way we organize our ministries contributes to such a fragmentation. Is your pastoral team spending time together, formally and informally? Does your church sponsor intergenerational activities, such as joint picnics, short-term missions and special worship services? Is God calling you to initiate something small in this area?

Build culture. Every church has its own distinct culture or cultures, and a healthy multigenerational household of God requires a healthy culture that promotes intergenerational ties and partnership. Does your church have distinct, separate cultures that promote further segregation among different people groups in your church? The good news is that an institutional culture can be reshaped; it's not as static or fixed as we often seem to think. By introducing a new set of values, practices and vision, Open Door Presbyterian Church has successfully constructed a new congregational culture that includes and embraces both first- and second-generation congregations. What are some new values, norms and rituals your leadership can introduce to your church?

Be Christlike. In his epistle to the church in Philippi, the apostle Paul pleads for unity in the church and specifically exhorts the Philippian Christians to be Christlike in practicing mutual submission and servanthood (Phil 2:1-11). In the Asian immigrant church context this means that the first-generation leadership does not insist on exercising the power that their traditional culture grants them. Rather, they choose to make room for their young people, inviting them to grow into leadership roles. This also means that second-generation young people, in turn, should respond by honoring their elders, thus setting up an ongoing cycle of mutuality and reciprocity between the two groups. How does your church address the issue of power and control? Do you approach and work out generational conflicts with an attitude of humility and servanthood of our Lord Jesus?

Clearly, building a healthy intergenerational relationship within the Asian immigrant church calls for much work and effort. Furthermore, putting in work does not necessarily guarantee its success; it can be a risky endeavor. However, this project is too critical, both theologically and sociologically, to be neglected by the Asian immigrant church. It is our sincere prayer and hope that many emerging pastoral and lay leaders will take this challenge seriously and prayerfully, willing to be used by God's Spirit to transform many of our churches into healthy, multigenerational households of God.

■   ■   ■

It's 4:00 p.m. Sunday afternoon at the Open Door Presbyterian Church. Members of the first-generation Korean-speaking congregation and the second-generation English-speaking congregation are gathering in the sanctuary for a special joint worship service. For most of them it has already been a long day at church, and yet as they fill the sanctuary, there is excitement in the air.

This day, both congregations are coming together to commission the church's first two full-time missionary families. What makes this event even more special for this twenty-year-old congregation is that both missionaries are second-generation young people who grew up in the church. The multigenerational participants of the worship service, using Korean and English, thank God for these young missionaries and fervently pray for their upcoming ministry in Uzbekistan. As the missionary candidates share their own stories, including their experiences growing up in this church, both young and old are deeply moved, expressing their emotions with tears as well as hearty laughter.

During this shared moment, members and leaders of these two congregations experience the joy and benefit of being a part of a larger family. As they pledge to pray for and to support these young missionary families, these two congregations implicitly also renew their commitment to their intergenerational partnership. As they celebrate this occasion of offering their "best" for the cause of Christ and world missions, members of both congregations acknowledge that these young missionaries and their families are the fruit of this congregation's past two decades of ministry. They gratefully reflect on their shared past and get a glimpse into the future ministry of these two families and of their multigenerational church, facing it with much hope and anticipation, for they are traveling together in this multigenerational household of God's people.

8

GENDER RELATIONS IN HEALTHY HOUSEHOLDS

PETER CHA AND GRACE MAY

"Your sons and daughters will prophesy."
ACTS 2:17

AS A GRADUATING SENIOR, CHRISTY WAS ELATED when multiple prestigious corporations offered her jobs. After prayerful deliberation, she decided to take the offer from the company that was located in her hometown, not because it offered the heftiest salary package but because, among other things, she wanted to return to her home church, a congregation that played a significant role in her life during her childhood and adolescence. Having received valuable training as a student leader of a thriving college ministry, Christy was especially excited about the possibility of helping with the launch of a second-generation young adult ministry.

Christy's homecoming experience, however, turned out to be a very ambivalent one. While the leaders and members of her home church warmly received her, they began to communicate to her what she could and could not do because she was a woman. In spite of her gifts and experience, she was discouraged from leading a co-ed Bible study group, serving as a member of the praise team or even teaching high school Sunday school classes.

The only ministry opportunities she was able to explore with the blessing of the church leadership were in the nursery and the children's program. After a period of struggles and frustration, Christy decided to leave her home church, a decision that was made with much reluctance and inner conflict.

Tragically, stories like this are repeated in many Asian and Asian American congregations. Recent studies that examined gender relations in Asian immigrant congregations noted that a strong ethos of gender hierarchy still governs the day-to-day practices within these communities. These studies also note that these values and practices are particularly offensive to second-generation women who are well-educated and have professional careers. Many, like Christy, may decide to leave their Asian congregations to find a church where they can fully exercise their gifts.

A healthy congregation, as a household of God, provides a safe and nurturing place for all of its members to grow as sons and daughters of God. It provides a sociocultural and spiritual environment in which its members can form healthy spiritual, ethnic and gender identities. In addition, such a congregation also provides a setting where its members can safely explore and develop all of the gifts that the Holy Spirit has sovereignly given to them, a community that encourages men and women to use their spiritual gifts to *serve one another* and *with one another* as co-laborers in Christ.

In this chapter we will first examine a number of cultural and historical barriers that frequently hinder Asian American churches from becoming such congregations and then identify some biblical and theological principles that might be helpful in overcoming these cultural barriers. Finally, we will look at the experiences of a number of Asian American congregations that are intentionally seeking to grow in this vital area, paying attention to the specific values and practices they embrace and employ.

CULTURE-SHAPED GENDER BIAS

As Asian Americans, we gratefully acknowledge the many positive traditions we have received from our forebears, but our traditional view of gender is not one of them. While women tend to be viewed as inferior in most traditional Asian societies, it is especially so among groups that are deeply influenced by centuries of Confucian teaching and practices. From its early years Confucianism emphatically taught that the hierarchical relationship between men and women was an important ethical mandate that should be firmly practiced in order to maintain order within families, communities and societies. Therefore, one of the cardinal Confucian principles, the Principle of the Three Bonds, teaches that "the ruler, the father and the husband are to be the standards of the ruled, the son and the wife" (Wing-Tsit Chan, *Source Book in Chinese Philosophy*). In the three vertical relationships, the superior partners were called "masters," and they were given complete control over their inferior partners.

In such a society, women did not have their own identity as persons. In traditional Asian society, women were often called so-and-so's daughter before marriage, so-and-so's wife after marriage, and so-and-so's mother after a son's birth. Their sense of being was very much reduced to the roles they played for others, particularly for the men in their lives. In many ways, women were viewed and treated as possessions or servants.

As Asian Americans, we may never have heard of the Principle of the Three Bonds or of other Confucian teachings on gender roles and relations. Nevertheless, we can readily see in our daily lives the cumulative effect of centuries of these teachings and practices. Today in America a godly Asian mother tells her daughter that it is not good for a woman to get too much education, because then a man will not want to marry her. In many Asian American families, mothers do not let sons do the dishes or other house chores, insisting that those tasks are to be done by daughters. These male-centered values and practices are found not just in our homes but in our churches; for these enduring cultural values shape not only Asian American individuals but also our communities.

AMERICAN EVANGELICALISM AND GENDER RELATIONS

In addition to traditional Asian culture, another significant factor that affects the Asian American churches' understanding of gender relations is the way

American evangelicalism has viewed and practiced gender roles in the church. Given their conservative theological orientation, the majority of Asian American congregations have, over the years, developed a strong relationship with the American evangelical community. As they have continually utilized resources produced by evangelical publishers and sent their future pastors to American evangelical seminaries, the tie between the Asian American Christian community and the broader evangelical community has been steadily reinforced. Thus many theological issues that have affected the broader American evangelical community have also profoundly influenced the Asian American Christian community, including the issue of gender.

Currently, the evangelical Christian community in North America is engaged in a heated—and often uncivil—debate on the role of women in church. Some evangelical churches prohibit women from exercising any teaching or leading gifts while others permit and encourage women to exercise these gifts in all contexts. While many theologians insist that this debate is purely theological or exegetical in nature, careful observation indicates that some of the trends in our culture and society significantly shape our discussion and perspectives on this issue.

Historical studies note that when the American evangelical church was expanding vibrantly during the nineteenth and the early part of the twentieth centuries, many denominations encouraged both men and women to exercise their spiritual gifts and leadership in the church. In addition to mainline denominations, theologically conservative denominations such as the Christian and Missionary Alliance, Evangelical Free Church of America, Church of the Nazarene, the Free Methodists, and various Baptist and Pentecostal denominations ordained women pastors until the 1930s. However, during the second half of the twentieth century, many evangelical denominations began to discourage women from seeking public ministry. Internally, as the evangelical church became more institutionalized and sought seminary-trained pastors, women were gradually pushed out of leadership roles. Externally, conservative churches reacted strongly to the growing visibility and threat of feminism in the wider culture. Convinced that the survival of traditional family values was at stake, many of these churches further discouraged women from engaging in public ministry, particularly from playing leadership roles.

In turn, with respect to gender concerns, the Asian American church mirrored the perspective of the wider American evangelical community. One sociologist who studied gender relations in Asian immigrant churches concluded that these churches tended to marginalize women by barring them from leadership roles and by denying them any significant voice in the community life. Another study that examined second-generation Asian American congregations noted that many of them continue to teach and practice gender hierarchy. These teachings and practices need to be biblically and critically reassessed by Asian American congregations.

SONS AND DAUGHTERS OF GOD

Our heavenly Father has both sons and daughters, and embraces and supports both. Beginning with the first chapter of Genesis, God unequivocally states that together men and women reflect the image of God. "In the image of God he created him, male and female he created them" (Gen 1:27). In the cultural mandate "God blessed *them,* and God said to *them,* 'Be fruitful and multiply, and fill the earth and subdue it'" (Gen 1:28, italics mine). The Lord commissioned Adam and Eve to jointly rule over the world, not to lord it over each other, but to relate harmoniously as equals. Rejoicing over the similarity he sees in her, Adam sings at Eve's creation, "bone of my bone and flesh of my flesh." By sharing one flesh, in their unity, the first couple reflects the oneness of God. God created human community to mirror the community that exists perfectly in the Godhead. In the fall, however, humanity, the crowning touch of God's creation, destroys both the community and the unity that God has graciously bestowed.

Adam and Eve's disobedience not only marred the image of God in each of them but fractured their relationship with each other and frustrated their rule of the earth. Instead of giving themselves in love to each other, they retreated into their own defensive and self-centered corners. Love and trust diminished as each denied responsibility for their own wrongdoing. As a result, they isolated themselves from one another and their Creator. Instead of joy over their creativity and productivity, their labor yielded "thorns and thistles" (Gen 3:18), producing pain and disappointment. Fraught with dissatisfaction, their work became a source of endless complaints. Argument and competition became the norm.

As God predicted, sin shattered the human community, and sexism entered the world, even prior to racism and classism. God already foresaw the battle of the sexes as it would be played out in unfair employment practices, domestic violence and sexual exploitation. At the same time God foreknew the victory that was at hand. Ultimately God's Son would restore the equality and the harmony that God originally intended. As early as Eden God prophetically declared that the "offspring," or "seed," of Eve would strike the head of the evil one, placing the hope of the human race neither on man nor woman, but on Christ (Gen 3:15).[1]

Thus began the redemptive stream of the Scriptures, a stream that expanded progressively and reached its apex in Christ. Christ's death and resurrection made possible the tearing down of barricades between genders, races and classes. The cross reconciles men and women to one another and offers them the ability to live beyond the curse and as co-heirs of Christ. Through the Great Commission, Jesus reinstated men and women as co-regents of the earth, sending them to disciple the nations of the world and baptizing them in the name of the Father, Son and Holy Spirit—the perfect model of community (Mt 28:18-19).

At the next watershed, Pentecost, God gave birth to the church. The apostle Peter described the nature of this new community by quoting the prophet Joel, who assured:

> In the last days, God says,
>   I will pour out my Spirit on all people.
> Your sons and daughters will prophesy. (Acts 2:17)

This new household of God will not be defined or dominated by one ethnicity, class or gender. Rather, it will be defined by the presence of the Holy Spirit working in and among his people. God calls both men and women to speak the truth, which is the very foundation of our faith. In God's new household, God's sons and daughters will declare the Lord's greatness by relating to one another in love, and fulfilling their responsibilities in a spirit of gratitude and humility. For God desires all his children, born of the Spirit and endowed with certain gifts, to live together as a royal priesthood, proclaiming his mighty acts to all the world (1 Pet 2:9).

Since the very beginning, God's original design was that men and women live in partnership. I (Grace) define partnership as a relationship between individuals and communities of believers that reflect the communion shared by the Triune. A study of *koinōnia,* the Greek word for "fellowship" or "community," reveals the depths of the sharing experienced by the early church. Believers fellowshiped daily over meals. (In 1 Corinthians 11:17-34, communion was celebrated as part of a potluck meal called the love feast.) They pooled material resources (which reduced the gap between the haves and the have-nots, e.g. Acts 4:32-37; Rom 12:13, 15:26; 2 Cor 8:4; 9:13; Phil 4:15; 1 Tim 6:18; Heb 13:16), they worked together as close friends and ministry partners (e.g. Phoebe and Paul, Aquila and Priscilla, and the long list in Rom 16), and they shared in Christ's suffering (e.g. 2 Cor 1:7; Phil 3:10; Heb 10:33; 1 Pet 4:13). When persecuting the church, Paul made no distinction between genders (see Acts 8:3).

The early church embodied the radical truth that there is "neither Jew nor Gentile, neither slave nor free, neither male nor female" (Gal 3:28). The life and ministry of the early church assumed that men and women, under Christ's authority, *served one another* and *served alongside one another* in God's household. It is in light of this shared assumption and the plethora of biblical examples of women leaders—Miriam, Deborah, Abigail, Huldah, Esther, Anna, Mary, Jesus' female disciples, Philip's four daughters, Lydia, Tabitha and Paul's many coworkers—that any difficult Pauline passages are to be read and interpreted.[2] The apostle Paul described Phoebe (Rom 16:1) using the same Greek word for "minister" (*diakonos*) that he uses for church leaders like Timothy and himself (1 Tim 4:6; Col 1:23). Similarly, he called attention to many prominent women, such as the apostle Junia (Rom 16:7) and Priscilla, who taught as part of a husband and wife team (Acts 18:2; Rom 16:3; 1 Cor 16:19; 2 Tim 4:19). Through the redemptive work of Christ and the empowering work of the Holy Spirit, men and women are now able to collaborate with one another in doing God's work, as God the Creator intended from the very beginning.

Currently, mirroring the wider evangelical Christian community, the Asian American church is divided on the issue of women's role in ministry. On the one hand, there are some congregations that affirm that men and women are not only equal in their being but also in the way they are to serve God and his church.[3] On the other hand, a majority of Asian American congregations acknowledge that while men and women are equal in being, women are not to participate in certain leadership and preaching or teaching roles in the church.[4] While the differences between these two positions cannot be easily overlooked or reconciled, we want to assert that all Asian American churches, in order to become healthy households of God, need to work on the important task of affirming both God's sons *and* daughters.

GENDER RELATIONS AND THE POSTMODERN WORLD

This truth is even more critical for the church in today's postmodern world. Postmoderns are not only familiar with the concept of the "hermeneutics of suspicion" but also are quite apt to use this hermeneutic to analyze their social surroundings, including their religious communities. According to Paul Little, the well-known evangelist of the 1960s, the following were some of the questions non-Christians asked most about Christianity at that time: Does God exist? Is Christianity scientific? Did Christ's resurrection really happen?[5] According to Rick Richardson, a leading evangelist in today's postmodern world, the following are some of the questions today's skeptics raise: Why do Christians impose their beliefs and morality on others? How can I trust the church that has done terrible things in the name of Christ? Doesn't the church legitimate certain hierarchical structures in our culture and society, including patriarchy?[6] We can readily see the differences between these two sets of questions. The former focuses on matters of doctrine while the latter pays attention to certain practices of churches, particularly on how the church uses (or misuses) its power and how it relates to certain groups of people, including women. In short, how the church treats women can greatly help or hinder its ability to witness in today's postmodern world.

This insight is especially critical to Asian American churches that are seeking to reach out to well-educated postmoderns. In many ways American-born Asian American women who feel marginalized in their traditional families are hesitant to stay with a church that seems to mimic their traditional cultural teaching of gender hierarchy. It's enough that women experience pain in their biological family; not many desire to repeat such experiences in their spiritual homes as well. Indeed, many Asian American Christian leaders observed that more women than men join the "Silent Exodus" from Asian churches. Ken Fong, in *Pursuing the Pearl*, laments:

> What does concern me is that many of the people we want to affect are quite comfortable with women, including Asian American women, being educated and professionals. When so many Asian American women have been reared to be assertive, independent, and competent, how can they fit into churches that relegate them to subservient, passive roles?[7]

Fong and other concerned Asian American pastors are convinced that the formation of healthy gender relations is one of the most critical tasks that face many Asian American congregations today because of how it affects their ministry of evangelism and discipleship. Thankfully, many emerging Asian American congregations are making intentional efforts to grow in this area and to become nurturing households for both men and women. In the rest of the chapter, we will explore some of the specific steps these congregations are taking to promote healthy gender relations.

THE PASTORAL TEAM IS KEY

Pastors play a very crucial role in the development of healthy gender relations in their congregations. As the pastoral staff goes, so goes the church. Do pastors appreciate and respect all of their church leaders, both men and women? Do they effectively shepherd all of God's children, both male and female, whom God has placed under their care? Do they model before their congregations a healthy friendship and partnership with individuals of different gender?

Since many Asian American pastors grew up in homes and churches where gender inequality and hierarchy were deeply rooted, the growth curve can be steep. The journey involves undoing years of cultural socialization, and replacing inherited attitudes and values with new ones. In short, it is a journey of personal transformation.

David Gibbons of the NewSong Church is one such Asian American pastor. Having grown up and been trained in a fundamentalist background, David felt strongly during his early years of ministry that women should be prohibited from preaching and certain leadership positions. However, during his years of pastoral ministry in the Korean immigrant church as well as in a multiethnic congregation, he started to wrestle with this perspective as he witnessed the hurt in women who were gifted to lead. He especially struggled with past applications he had made from the Scriptures regarding women. Soon David began to encourage women to use their gifts to serve the church and bring glory to God. These experiences in turn encouraged David to study the Scriptures more deeply, examining various interpretations of the passages that deal with women's role in ministry and other related issues. Through his studies he came to the conclusion that the Scriptures not only permit but also strongly encourages both men and women to *identify*, to *steward* and to *express their spiritual gifts*—including those of teaching and leading—in the household of God. Today, David is working alongside many gifted sisters and brothers who are fully employing their God-given gifts to further God's kingdom.

Such a personal journey of growth and transformation, however, is not just for male leaders of the church. Given that traditional Asian cultural values affect both genders, Asian American women Christian leaders also need to embark on a journey, albeit a slightly different one. Nancy Sugikawa, a pastor of the Lighthouse Christian Church in Seattle, had to overcome many cultural and theological barriers to embrace her own calling from God. Having grown up in a traditional Asian home and in a conservative Southern Baptist church, Nancy never envisioned that she would one day serve as a pastor. Yet Nancy vividly remembers listening to visiting women missionaries with intense interest as a young child. Even at an early age Nancy wondered who would do the baptizing and discipling of men and women if there were no male pastors in many mission fields.

During her college years at Berkeley, Nancy began to get involved in ministry, particularly focusing on the ministry of discipling other women. After graduation, while working as an engineer, Nancy continued her active engagement in ministry, this time as a Japanese American lay person in the church. She loved working with young adults who were very motivated to grow but was also deeply frustrated because they could not find male pastors to teach them. The experience left a deep impression on her. Years later, she reflected:

> Our monthly young adult services were a hit, but our greatest obstacle was finding pastors to speak for us. One month I had run out of options and knelt before God crying out, "God, you have to send us a preacher! People are so hungry spiritually but there is no food for them!" Then I suddenly heard God say to me, "You give them something to eat." But I said, "No, Lord, I don't have any food to give them. I can't preach." And then God said to me, "Then go and get trained."

However, given her theological and cultural upbringing, even after hearing such a clear mandate from God, Nancy hesitated. For a period of time she struggled with doubts and went to several individuals whom she respected, seeking their counsel. However, when it became very clear that God was indeed calling her to the vocation of ministry, Nancy left her engineering career and entered seminary. Today she is serving as a pastor of a vibrant and growing Asian American congregation, working with and serving both men and women. Pastors such as David and Nancy are transformed leaders because of the journey God led them through; they represent a new generation of Asian American evangelical leaders who intentionally help their congregations to grow as a nurturing and affirming place for all God's children, including women.

Like individual leaders, many Asian American congregations also corporately journey to grow and change in the area of gender relations. Two or three decades ago it would have been very difficult to find women pastors serving in Asian American congregations, including those that belong to so-called mainline denominations. But the situation is changing today. Recognizing that men and women bring different gifts and perspectives to the team, many Asian American churches are beginning to invite women to join their pastoral team. Today, churches such as the Evergreen Baptist Church of Los Angeles, NewSong Church, Cambridge Community Fellowship Church and Lighthouse Christian Church have women pastoral staff members who carry out all pastoral duties, including preaching and teaching.

Even churches that do not believe in ordaining women, such as Open Door Presbyterian Church, are inviting women to join their pastoral team. While they may not allow women to preach or teach in the congregational context, these churches are empowering their women pastors to exercise their leadership in their particular areas of ministry. What is important to note is that a church like Open Door Presbyterian Church recognizes and addresses their women pastoral staff members as "pastors," not as "directors." Open Door Presbyterian Church sets high standards of respect for its leaders, both male and female, and seeks to grow in its ability to affirm all God's children, including women, and their God-given gifts.

Finally, for those congregations that have both men and women on their pastoral staff, it is critical that the *team models healthy gender relations*. Given the prevailing cultural force that privileges male over female, male leaders need to take initiative in showing respect for their female colleagues. Nancy appreciates how her senior pastor, Wayne Ogimachi, seeks to do this for her and the women elders in her church. She noted:

> Wayne intentionally takes extra steps to give me visibility by calling me "Pastor Nancy," asking me to do the opening prayer at a leaders' gathering and having me participate in baptisms. He does the same with the two women elders, introducing them as elders at our newcomers' welcome luncheons.

As an ordained pastor, I (Grace) too appreciate when my male colleagues address me as Pastor Grace or Reverend May in public. In fact, some of my male colleagues who do not believe in women's ordination consistently introduce me by my title. Such an act signals to me their respect and beautifully demonstrates their Christian humility. It is as if they are saying, "You may be wrong or I may be wrong on the issue of women's ordination, but I will not let our theological differences on this matter keep me from treating you with respect and civility." Such an act of respect and humility, we believe, can powerfully reshape attitudes of the people and the culture of our congregations.

TRANSFORMATION THROUGH THE WORD

As Bible-believing Christians, we are people of the Book. We believe that the Word of God should guide and direct not only our individual lives but also our corporate life together as the church. Furthermore, we believe that the Word of God should serve as the standard against which we measure and assess all human cultures. The Bible assists us in identifying and affirming those elements of our culture that are redemptive, and convicts us to reject or transform those aspects that are sinful and harmful. Among the many dominant cultural values we inherited from our ancestors, strong gender hierarchy is one value that needs to be challenged and transformed for the health of Asian American families, communities and churches. This, we believe, is one of the important contributions the Asian American church can make. And the main tool that needs to be employed toward this end is the transformative Word of God.

Therefore, pastors directly and indirectly need to regularly address the topic of healthy gender relations in their teaching and preaching ministry. A pastor can preach about the power of the cross that restores unity and peace between men and women and about God's expansive vision for service in the kingdom. Sermons can highlight faithful women and men in the Scriptures and their unique contributions to God's kingdom. Pastors need to continually remind their church members that their heavenly Father calls each of them—black or white, rich or poor, weak or strong, male or female—his beloved. Asian American women who grew up feeling less valued by their parents because of their gender particularly need to hear that their heavenly Father does not view them as "less than." This is significant since our individual identities and our sense of worth are continuously shaped by how significant persons in our lives view and relate to us.

In sermons, pastors need to regularly encourage and affirm all members to identify their gifts and use them appropriately. A number of Asian American pastors who contributed to this book noted that capable and godly Asian American women are often reluctant to assume leadership roles; therefore church leaders may need to invite women to serve as leaders. The pastoral team of the Lighthouse Christian Church, for example, is very intentional about preaching periodically on the theme of women in ministry. Although the team includes a woman pastor, senior pastor Wayne Ogimachi preaches on this topic because it may seem self-serving for the woman pastor to do so, and also because he wants to communicate how important this matter is to him and to the whole congregation.

Given the many cultural and theological controversies surrounding women in church leadership, this particular topic may require in-depth biblical study and reflection beyond the scope of a thirty-minute sermon. When I (Peter) was serving at an Asian American congregation, we encountered some challenging moments as conflicting views of women's role in ministry collided with one another. Some felt that women should not be allowed to lead even small group Bible studies, while others felt that women should be able to serve in all levels of ministry in the church. As a way of addressing this growing division, we decided to invite a New Testament scholar from a nearby seminary to give us a full day's teaching on this and other related topics. More than half of the church members came out that day and participated in this exercise, listening attentively as well as asking many thoughtful questions.

After the full day exercise the church commissioned a group of leaders to draft a document that would explain our church's position on the issue. The team, consisting of both pastoral and lay leaders, went through many drafts, constantly seeking and receiving feedback from the congregation. The process of completing and ratifying this document as the church's official position paper was a lengthy and arduous one; however, it was also a valuable learning experience for our young congregation. In the end it deepened the church's understanding of this controversial issue and also helped us to identify a common ground for the congregation, whose members come from a variety of church traditions.

Reassessing Cultural Gender Roles in the Church

In addition to sound biblical and theological teachings, a healthy congregation should introduce practices and routines that promote healthy gender relations in its context. In many Asian homes, men and women play distinct roles: women wash, clean and take care of the children while men are often ridiculed if they engage in such activities. Such culturally shaped practices are found not only in our homes but in churches. In many Asian immigrant churches, men discuss various issues in the boardroom while women are busy in the kitchen, cooking meals for the entire congregation and cleaning up afterward. Men and women are expected to participate in these particular activities simply because they are women or men. Such practices allow cultural norms to prevail over biblical norms in shaping gender relations in the life of the church.

The need to thoughtfully reassess culturally constructed gender roles in the life of the church is particularly critical as we nurture children in the church. Social psychologists point out that the nurturing of healthy children requires the active presence of both fathers and mothers, of male and female adult role models. Many recent studies point to the unique and substantial contributions fathers and male role models make in the nurturing of both boys and girls, particularly in the area of developing healthy gender identities. Consequently, any healthy household of God that takes seriously the task of raising young children needs to find ways to involve both men and women in this ministry.

Yet, in most Asian American churches, the task of caring for young children is usually seen as women's work. In many Asian American congregations young mothers often can't participate in the worship service because they are caring for their own young children. In others, a small group of women are designated as nursery volunteers or as teachers for the children's department. Such practices contribute not only to burnout among these dedicated women but also raise a number of educational concerns as well. What would happen if men as well as women were encouraged and trained to serve in the nursery and lead children's program? What would happen if the pastor, when he does not preach on a given Sunday, serves in the nursery, communicating to the male members that caring for young children is not exclusively women's responsibility? What would happen if young children grew up in the family of God where numerous spiritual uncles and aunts knew them by name and generously expressed love and care for them?

At the Grace Community Covenant Church in Los Altos, a group of men who had a burden for young children took the plunge and started leading junior worship service for fifty to sixty children, seven years old and under. The task of planning and leading children's worship and of interacting constantly with young children is not easy work, especially for busy professionals. It also doesn't help that such work is often seen as women's work in many Asian American settings, including the church. However, convinced that these young children need the nurturing presence of spiritual uncles as well as aunts, they sacrificially invested their time in this new ministry. In doing so, they played a critical role not only in raising a new generation of Christians but also in transforming their own congregational culture.

STEPS TO TAKE

Given the cultural and theological backgrounds from which many of us come, developing healthy gender relations in our congregational context will require time and intentionality; it will be a long journey for many of us. The stories and experiences of the Asian American pastors and their congregations featured in this chapter point to that reality. We want to assert that this journey is relevant not just to those churches who welcome sisters in all areas of ministry. A growing number of churches that limit teaching and preaching to brothers are also growing in their ability to affirm their sister leaders and members, respecting, valuing and appreciating them. We are encouraged and are grateful to God for the positive changes we see, for the work God's Spirit is doing in our midst.

As a pastor or a lay leader, perhaps you are also sensing God's prompting to be stretched in this area. As you examine your congregational life, you see that there are many areas in which healthier gender relations can be promoted and practiced. However, where do you begin? What particular steps might be helpful for you and your congregation? We would like to propose a number of concrete action steps.

Carefully and prayerfully study the issue. Many of us realize that the Bible's treatment of gender roles is not as black and white as we thought. Having grown up in a very conservative Presbyterian church, I (Peter) believed that the Bible strictly prohibited women from engaging in any public ministry, including reading the Scriptures during the worship service. Then, when I attended Trinity Evangelical Divinity School and sat under the teachings of respected theologians such as Walter Kaiser and Kenneth Kantzer, I realized that there are other biblically supportable and convincing perspectives on this topic. Thankfully, there are many recently published resources that can help and guide your study.[8] This issue affects the entire congregation, not just women; it requires the serious attention of all church leaders, pastoral and lay.

Value all God's people as he would value each person. The Bible makes it very clear that our heavenly Father loves each child regardless of the person's ethnicity, socioeconomic status and gender, and calls Christians to love one another as he has loved us (1 Jn 4:7-21). As Christian leaders it is an important part of our pastoral duty to continuously communicate and model the truth that our Father values all his children equally and express this truth in the ways we carry out our ministry.

Critically analyze congregational practices. We need to critically and biblically assess not only what we believe but also what we do, for the latter shapes the church members as much as the former does. Do your practices follow Asian cultural norms in privileging males or do they follow the kingdom norms in valuing all God's children, including women?

Practice "ethics of care." An ethic of care recognizes the unfortunate social reality of inequality and encourages us to provide more care and support for those who are marginalized. In a typical Asian American congregation this means that the leadership needs to develop sensitivity and awareness to the particular needs and concerns of women since they are not often represented in the leadership. This also means that men take initiative in empowering and affirming their sisters in Christ, particularly in decision-making processes.

Say no to avoiding conflict at all cost. Our cultural tendency is to avoid conflict and simply ignore those issues that can cause conflict. But conflict avoidance is injurious to the health of your congregation because, by default, it allows traditional Asian gender relations and norms to guide your congregational life. Instead, your congregation needs to prayerfully and courageously study this issue together and find a shared position. This is particularly important for newly planted churches.

Improve cross-gender communication skills. Most married couples would confess that cross-gender communication is very challenging and can be fraught with misunderstanding and confusion. This is even more so in the larger context of the congregational life. Women in leadership positions, including pastors, must not excuse themselves from their responsibility to speak up and to express their concerns with clarity. They can learn to be more assertive as the occasion calls for it. At the same time men can also ask for clarification or grow in sensitivity to what is subtle and implicit. They should ask their sisters questions that will help men to understand. Undoubtedly there are wise people in your church who are especially good at processing and communicating, individuals who could serve well as counselors, intermediaries or sounding boards (e.g., women who have years of experience working with men in the marketplace, and men who have grown up with older and younger sisters in their families). There is no shame in reading practical how-to books on communication or in taking classes regarding these issues. The church and the world are replete with resources, if we know how to harness them for the kingdom.

The collaboration of men and women on joint projects and new paradigms for ministry could unleash a creative force and generate a revival on a scale that the world has yet to see. Jesus' prayer for unity (Jn 17:21) directly counters the spirit of divisiveness and competition unleashed by the serpent in the Garden. All of the enemy's efforts to thwart the redemptive and sovereign plan of God fall flat in the face of sisters and brothers working and dwelling together in unity. What could bring our Creator God more pleasure than seeing his children living as one family? And how much more do the chances of that happening grow as men and women serve together, embrace one another's gifts, respect and submit to one another? May our Father in heaven be glorified as emerging Asian American churches become households of God in which his sons and daughters live and serve in harmony, love and grace.

9

HOUSEHOLDS OF
MERCY AND JUSTICE
SOONG-CHAN RAH

IN EVERY SENSE, "JIMMY" IS A SPECIAL-NEEDS KID. Diagnosed as severely ADHD, this nine year-old-boy needs to be medicated three times a day. At school, he is in a program for kids with emotional and behavioral needs. He is the third child in a family of six children who live in Dorchester, a high crime, inner-city neighborhood in Boston. His parents are Haitian immigrants who work long hours at menial jobs to provide for the family. Jimmy is a prime candidate for being a street-running gangbanger—the kind of kid you cross the street to avoid, the kind of kid who ends up on a police report and then as a statistic, another child gone wrong in our inner cities.

It was not a shock, therefore, when I received a tearful phone call from his mother. Jimmy was in the hospital. He had assaulted his teacher and the school had committed him to the Cambridge Hospital for psychiatric evaluation. When my wife and I went to visit him, Jimmy looked distressed and frightened. He cried that he didn't want to be locked up in a hospital and wanted to go home. His mother seemed overwhelmed, unable to communicate clearly with the hospital staff and feeling the pain and distress of her child. She needed the church to be there for her and her son.

Jimmy's father works eighty hours per week as an orderly at two hospitals, and Jimmy's mother works thirty hours per week as a nurse's aide at Vernon Hall, a nursing home that members of the Cambridge Community Fellowship Church (Cambridge, Mass.) have been visiting since the inception of the church. Over the years the church has ministered to lonely, nursing-center-bound senior citizens at Vernon Hall. An unexpected outcome of our ministry has been meeting the Haitian nurses' aides who would occasionally join our times of worship with the Vernon Hall residents. Many of these nurses' aides are Christians who have not been in a church in a long time, and our times of worship served as their church.

Through Vernon Hall, we met Jimmy's mother, "Val." She asked us to pray for her family. When we held our first vacation Bible school, it was natural to ask Val if she wanted to send her kids. Four of her kids came to VBS, and the church counselors loved these wonderful kids. But we found that loving troubled kids for a week was the easy part. The hard part was following up and committing to their lives so that they don't end up as mere statistics. Jimmy's problems were not minor challenges that could be addressed by a week of songs, skits and field trips. He needed intensive care from his church family. Our church would need to become that family.

As a young Christian in high school called to ministry, I envisioned what church ministry would look like. I often thought about preaching to large crowds, laying hands on the sick and performing the sacraments. Now I see ministry as spending time with an at-risk youth, visiting hospitals and nursing homes, going to district court to help a family in trouble. I used to see church as a place where fun people gathered and the worship service was a neat presentation that provided an hour of entertainment for easily bored and distracted yuppies. Now church is everyday mundane activity. Church is a gathering of a dozen senior citizens and their caregivers. Church is a hospital room where a distressed mother and child have no one to turn to but their church family. Church is a home where discord and stress have brought a family to its breaking point. Church is a kid like Jimmy, whose lips form the most absurd curses for a nine-year-old boy, but whose eyes speak of a sincere desire to be loved.

Our churches need to be places where God's justice and mercy are proclaimed and demonstrated. If our churches are to become the household of God, then they must have a public witness and not merely exist for the sake of maintaining their own households.

Social justice and compassion ministry flows out of the mercy and grace that has been shown the household of God. Picture a glass of water that has been standing still for several days. After a while, that water becomes stale and putrid. Living water flows and moves. If the household of God is to be a living, growing, healthy community, then the life received from God must flow outward. How can Asian American churches address social injustices and the burgeoning needs of our society through compassion and mercy ministries? How will the emerging Asian American Christian community move out of its place of apathy and comfort to be a transformational force in our neighborhoods? How will our churches engage the "Jimmys" of our neighborhoods?

BIBLICAL AND THEOLOGICAL FOUNDATIONS

In my senior year in high school, I visited a school in New York City that would become my college alma mater. Having grown up a quintessential suburban community, the experience of the big city was overwhelming. I remember returning home to my church youth group and reporting to a shocked audience that I had actually seen two homeless people during my three days in New York. I remember remarking how unsafe the streets of Harlem (actually Morningside Heights) seemed. By the time I graduated from college, my view of the city had drastically changed. Some of the transformation was due to the social reality that instead of seeing two homeless people in a three-day period, I was now accustomed to seeing scores of homeless people on a daily basis—the issues of poverty and economic injustice were staring me directly in the face.

Not only was I faced with the realities of social injustice in an urban setting, I was being exposed to biblical teaching that spoke to the issue of injustice. Much of my early Christian formation had been in the context of churches that had focused on individual spirituality, sometimes to the exclusion of a corporate application of Scripture. During my college years, my involvement with my campus InterVarsity Christian Fellowship chapter provided me with challenges from Scripture to seek God's justice and reconciliation. Since then I have sought teaching, books, Scripture studies and mentors who have opened the Bible to me, not only as an expression of God's love to the individual but to the world. The Bible is not silent on the issue of social justice and compassion. The church must be led to an understanding that a healthy and holistic household of God requires an application of the biblical mandate for ministries of justice and mercy.

In the book *Kingdom Ethics* we learn that "by a conservative count, the four words for justice . . . appear 1,060 times in the Bible."[1] Jim Wallis informs us, "In the Old Testament, the suffering of the poor was the second most prominent theme. . . . In the New Testament we found that one out of every sixteen verses was about the poor. In the Gospels, it was one out of every ten; in Luke, one of every seven; and in James, one of every five verses."[2] A member of the Sojourners community in Washington D.C. tried an experiment. "He found an old Bible and a pair of scissors, and he cut out of that Bible every single reference to the poor. . . . When he was all through, the Bible was literally in shreds. It wouldn't hold together; it was falling apart in our hands. . . . [T]his is the American Bible—full of holes."[3]

The book of Genesis provides the initial thread of understanding the social implication of the gospel. In Genesis 1:27 we find that humanity is created in the image of God. This image is reflected not only in the individual but also through the creation of both male and female. The tricolon parallelism in this verse shows that being created male and female is a part of being made in the image of God. The interdependence, mutual need and community found in the male-female dichotomy is a reflection of the unity found in the diversity of the Trinity. Humanity, reflecting the image of God, therefore should not be limited to an individual expression but needs to be understood in the social dimension as well.

Throughout the Pentateuch the call for holiness is applied to a social dimension. Deuteronomy 10:18-19 reminds the people of God that "He defends the cause of the fatherless and the widow, and loves the foreigners residing among you, giving them food and clothing. And you are to love those who are foreigners, for you yourselves were foreigners in Egypt." The book of Leviticus has numerous examples of the connection between holiness and concern for the poor (Lev 19:10; 23:22; 25:35).

The poetical and prophetical books repeatedly address social injustices and call Israel to exhibit justice and mercy as part of their identity as the people of God. Psalm 14:6 ("the LORD is their refuge"), 34:6 ("the LORD heard him") and 68:10 ("God . . . provided for the poor") reveal God's concern for the poor. Psalm 82:3 ("Defend the cause of the weak and fatherless; / uphold the cause of the poor and oppressed") and Proverbs 14:31 ("whoever is kind to the needy honors God") shows that God's concern for the poor demands a like response from his people. Prophets assert strong statements regarding God's concern for justice: "Let justice roll on like a river, / righteousness like a never-failing stream" (Amos 5:24), and

> Take your evil deeds
>> out of my sight!
> Stop doing wrong,
>> learn to do right!
> Seek justice,
>> encourage the oppressed.
> Defend the cause of the fatherless,
>> plead the case of the widow. (Is 1:16-17)

In the New Testament, Jesus' self-proclaimed purpose and identity derives from the Isaianic quotation given in Luke 4:18:

> The Spirit of the LORD is on me,
>> because he has anointed me
>> to proclaim good news to the poor.

Jesus' teachings reflect the kingdom value of concern for the poor and the oppressed. When an expert of the law approaches Jesus with a question about eternal life (Lk 10), he responds with the parable of the good Samaritan. Jesus' answer calls for an individual response, but individual salvation seems to have a social implication and application. The parable of the good Samaritan reveals Jesus' concern that those in the kingdom should reflect the kingdom value of mercy and compassion. The parable helps us see that the physical needs of the world are not to be ignored, but rather we are to see a new definition of "neighbor," yielding a ministry of compassion that engages the world.

In the same way, Jesus' final charge to the apostles in Acts 1:8 shows his concern for the world. Jesus commands us to be "my witnesses in Jerusalem, and in all Judea and Samaria, and to the ends of the earth." Often, in our great hurry to take the message to the ends of the earth, we neglect the needs found in Samaria. Jesus commands his people to be the bearers of his justice and mercy to our churches, our neighborhoods, our cities, our nations and our world. Will we take seriously the challenge of Scripture to be those who exhibit God's justice and mercy?

JUSTICE AND MERCY IN THE IMMIGRANT CHURCH CONTEXT

The Asian American church emerges out of the immigrant experience. The *anomie* felt by those transplanted from their home culture to the unfamiliar culture of America often provides the context in which immigrant churches can flourish. Immigrants flock to churches to recover primary relationships lost in the process of immigration. Immigrant parents, unfamiliar and wary of their surrounding culture, will seek to preserve their culture and shield their children from external influences. Christian parents, wary of their surrounding culture will also seek to shield their children from external influences. Immigrant Christian communities, therefore, are vigilant in their focus on preserving the spiritual well-being of the second generation, often to the exclusion of engaging secular culture.

The Korean church of my youth was geared toward the salvation of the children of the immigrant generation. Summertime meant numerous revival meetings and retreats aimed at the personal experience of salvation for the individual. Engagement with the hostile foreign culture and the temptations endemic in the culture were discouraged. I recall hearing a sermon explaining the architecture of our church's building. The church was one of the first church structures built by an immigrant community in the region. If you looked up in the sanctuary, the ceiling of the church was curved as if you were looking up at the hull of an upside-down boat. The architecture was meant to reflect the perspective that the church was like Noah's Ark—providing sanctuary for the saved and protection from the judgment that was falling on the outside world.

For many churches emerging out of the immigrant community, the felt needs within the community are paramount. Often, concern for individual salvation and personal evangelism of those within the ethnic community are given priority. The emerging Asian American church needs to recognize the strong tendency within the immigrant church toward a personalized and even a marginalized faith journey.

MINISTRY OF EDUCATION

Education can be a key element of change in the Asian American context. To become a church that exhibits God's justice and compassion, Asian American churches must begin by transforming the worldview of its congregations. Our churches must grow in the knowledge that expressing God's justice, compassion and mercy are an integral part of God's Word and part of God's mandate for his church. Many in our churches will find this paradigm shift to be a challenge to their basic Christian worldview.

When NewSong Church (Irvine, Calif.) wanted to initiate a compassion and justice ministry on a congregationwide scale, Pastor David Gibbons explored these themes from the pulpit through a study of Scripture. Congregations need to see that these truths arise from a Scripture rather than as a response to cultural trends. Through the sermon series the congregation found the biblical and theological conviction to pursue ministries of justice and reconciliation. At the close of the sermon series Gibbons took a strong stand and spoke of his desire to pastor a church that would take these words seriously. Similarly, Pastor Ken Fong's frequent emphasis on teaching biblical truths about justice and compassion from the pulpit provides a significant part of the motivation for Evergreen Baptist Church of Los Angeles' (Rosemead, Calif.) strong emphasis on justice ministries.

There are numerous obstacles to justice and compassion ministry that must be addressed from a corporate level at the church. Rampant individualism in our culture requires that a biblical understanding of God's concern for social justice be addressed from the pulpit. A pulpit emphasis, small group studies or a specific Sunday school class on the biblical mandate for justice and compassion are critical in a church's development and growth in justice and compassion ministries. It is also imperative that the church leadership have a commitment to understanding the biblical and theological foundations for justice and mercy. Many Asian Americans come from theologically sound but socially conservative churches. Plunging into justice and mercy ministries without strong scriptural teaching may cause many in the congregation to resist what some may consider a part of a more liberal tradition.

MINISTRY OF VALUES TRANSFORMATION

Educating the congregation on the biblical values of justice and compassion is a crucial first step. However, if these values are not internalized and the value systems of the individual and the congregation are not transformed, then the teaching will merely result in knowledge without practice. The transformation of the value system begins with education but continues with the shaping of the church's identity, mission and vision.

A shift in a church's value system should be reflected in a balance between internal and external ministry—reaching both those within and outside the church. Cambridge Community Fellowship Church has identified seven core values: Scripture, worship and prayer, community, witness, racial reconciliation, urban ministry and social justice, and world mission. Each of these values are woven into the fabric of church life. The church recognized, however, that attention must be focused on the values that have been neglected within evangelicalism—racial reconciliation and social justice. From the church's first service, Cambridge Community Fellowship Church has emphasized a ministry of justice and reconciliation. The teaching from the pulpit, discussion in small groups and available ministry opportunities stressed the transformation of the believer's values to reflect biblical values in a more balanced way.

As our churches strive to become the household of God, we'll begin to see that being the household of God requires the transformation of the individual believer. To invite someone into the household of God means to invite him or her into a loving relationship with the head of this household, Jesus Christ. As one enters this household the value system of that household begins to influence the individual. The community that develops in the household of God experiences a value transformation that reshapes the individual believer. As the household of God transforms the value system of the believer, the way the believer lives out his or her faith in the world is now transformed. Then the transformed individual can influence and transform the world. Evangelism is no longer defined simply as individual salvation but can now be seen as the expression of God's kingdom values into the world as expressed by the household of God.

MINISTRY WITHIN YOUR CHURCH

Justice and compassion ministries can begin with the immediate needs found within your congregation. Initially, many in the congregation may be more willing to work within their own church context than crossing cultural and socioeconomic barriers. This approach will also appeal to those who would take a more literal interpretation of the Great Commission (Mt 28:18-20)—seeking to be witnesses first in Jerusalem (Acts 1:8). This approach may also open the eyes of the congregation to social and economic needs within the community that may have not been previously noticed. When people do justice and compassion ministry in their own church context, it may expand their heart for ministry to those who are suffering outside of the church. Political and social stances that may have become calloused due to ignorance may be softened. Living out the value of mercy and justice within the church community may make ministering God's mercy and justice outside the church community more credible.

HARBOR (Help And Benevolence OutReach) ministry at Lighthouse Christian Church was initiated by several men's groups that saw the trials and difficulties of single moms and widows within their congregation. These men's groups and others from the church give one Saturday morning each month to provide basic services such as yard work, house cleaning and home and car repairs. HARBOR provides a service to members of the church community that is readily translated to those with particular needs outside of the church community. An act of service geared toward church members can become an act of servant evangelism toward nonmembers.

Despite the inward focus of most immigrant churches, Asian American churches have within its ecclesiastical DNA the potential for outward expressions of compassion and justice ministry. In addition to evangelistic zeal focused on their own people group, immigrant churches also provide a significant amount of social services to those in the church. My widowed, single-parent cousin transitioned fairly quickly and easily to life in the United States because a local Korean church rallied to her aid—helping her find a place to live, helping her to land a job, and helping her with her immigration paperwork. The Korean immigrant church demonstrated compassion toward an individual within its own community. The ministry of the immigrant church, therefore, can serve as a model or precursor to outward expressions of justice and compassion.

Ministry of Partnership

When justice and compassion ministry begins to venture beyond the confines of the immediate church community, authentic and reciprocal partnerships must be established to strengthen credibility and effectiveness. This concern is particularly relevant to many of our churches that may not worship in the places of need. Pastor Gibbons of NewSong Church met with key leaders in the African American community before initiating community outreach in urban Los Angeles. These conversations and the subsequent relationships that developed were meant to honor the existing work of the African American churches in the community. NewSong sought the blessing of these key church leaders before initiating outreach into these neighborhoods. Evergreen Baptist Church-LA partners with several local churches in conducting neighborhood outreach. There are several ways to develop significant partnerships with both church and parachurch ministries.

Grace Community Covenant Church is located in the affluent Silicon Valley suburb of Los Altos. Because of its location, the need for a ministry of justice and compassion in the church's neighborhood is not readily evident. Having a strong sense of financial stewardship, the church has committed to give at least 50 percent of the church's income externally. Two teams—the Global Compassion Team and Community Involvement Team—are charged with determining potential partners in justice and compassion ministries. Careful criteria, such as the potential for long-term partnerships, have been established in order to insure that any financial support would be a means of developing genuine partnerships. Research into potential partnerships and the developing of relationships to affirm those partnerships provide critical connections for the development of justice and compassion ministry.

Partnering with another ministry can also take the form of providing human resources in addition to or in lieu of financial resources. Well-established social ministries provide a great starting point for justice and compassion ministry. Churches (like Lighthouse Christian Church) can partner with established organizations like Habitat for Humanity by providing human resources. Soup kitchens and homeless shelters in the region provide an outlet for many in the congregation who are seeking ways to minister justice and compassion. Cambridge Community Fellowship Church partnered with Leon de Juda, a Spanish-speaking congregation, to develop a mentoring program for HERC (Higher Education Resource Center). HERC provides tutoring, support and resources for underprivileged high school students to help them apply to colleges. Over the years Cambridge Community Fellowship Church has also partnered with several African American churches and ministries, particularly those working with at-risk youth. When the urban-youth gang problem expanded to include Southeast Asians, the church's relationships with these ministries led to the creation of a ministry reaching out to Vietnamese gang youth.

There is also the possibility that justice and compassion ministries may yield partnerships with a broader coalition of agencies. For example, Evergreen Baptist Church-LA has worked with a secular organization that serves the needs of drug addicts. Partnering with non-Christian organizations can create outreach into the community that may otherwise be unavailable. Of course, each church must establish parameters and their threshold of tolerance in working with agencies and ministries across ethnic, cultural, denominational and even faith differences.

MINISTRY OF INCARNATION

The ministry of education, values transformation, service within the church and partnerships will often lead to a greater sense of need for incarnational ministry. As individuals in the church have firsthand experience working with the poor and the marginalized, many will desire deeper involvement in the community. As values are being transformed and individuals are experiencing the joy of serving—and being served—many will want to do more. The call to live out God's justice in the world will be stirring enough that they will radically rethink the basic definitions of discipleship. Sporadic inner-city visits may be unsatisfying. It seems too distant and too disconnected to have a long-term effect. As churches deepen their involvement and commitment, a healthy hunger will emerge to be a type of church where ministry to the poor is a daily part of life.

Most churches will begin as justice and compassion ministry "tourists"—seeing how justice ministry is being carried out by others. But values transformation and ministry partnerships can move a church to becoming more of a "participant/observer" in seeking to address social injustices. Then, individuals and even a church itself can begin to move from the first two stages to becoming "resident aliens," that is, actually moving into impoverished neighborhoods. The transition from participant/observer to resident alien may be the most difficult one. Pastor Steve Wong of Grace Community Covenant Church notes that as his church seeks to move through these stages, questions about housing choices, the impact on children's lives, and safety and education issues all emerge. Churches, of course, will need to determine what stage of involvement they willing to embrace. Even choosing to stay at a certain level below resident alien will mean sharpening and deepening that level of involvement. For example, a suburban church may decide to operate on the tourist level, but may seek ways to deepen its connection and involvement in urban settings by creating programs of advocacy that would use its resources to address various social injustices. (But as is often the case, as the awareness and interest in justice and compassion ministry increases, the push toward becoming a resident alien will also increase.)

In developing incarnational ministry, various models can be examined. Churches can look at models proposed by John Perkins and the Christian Community Development Association (CCDA). They emphasize the three Rs of community development: relocation, reconciliation and redistribution. Relocation calls for living among the poor and sharing their suffering, pain and joy; it "transforms 'you, them, and theirs' into 'we, us, and ours.' " Reconciliation seeks to "break down every racial, ethnic, or economic barrier. . . . As Christians come together . . . to partner and witness together across these barriers." Redistribution occurs "when God's people with resources are living in the poor in the community and are a part of it, applying the skills and resources to the problems of that community."[4] Churches should learn more about communities of need and attempt to become an authentic part of those communities, churches that don't merely *meet* in the neighborhood but actually become *part of* the neighborhood. Churches can become more involved in specific neighborhoods by developing urban-suburban partnerships through community organizing and political advocacy. Creative approaches will need to be developed to create a sense of deeper involvement in the local neighborhood and community.

Evergreen Baptist Church-LA initiated a novel campaign to increase involvement by the congregants in their local neighborhood. The church gave out fifty $100 bills to various individuals and small groups. Their charge was to be an answer to someone's prayer over the next ten weeks. One group chose to throw a party for wayward boys, and another group threw a Valentine's Day party for a halfway house for women. Out of these one-time efforts, congregants began to find ministry in their neighborhood. Testimonies stemming from this campaign showed that the congregation was beginning to rethink how their resources could serve the ongoing needs of their community. Through this campaign, the church began to get a glimpse of becoming more actively involved in their neighborhood.

After working on transforming the value system of Cambridge Community Fellowship Church, various members began to be more intentional about engaging the community. More members began to move into the immediate neighborhood of Central Square, where the church is located. The church is seeking to develop house-church communities and outreach programs that will become an integral part of the Central Square neighborhood. Children's programs focus outreach on the specific neighborhood and intentional partnerships are developed with churches within several blocks of the Cambridge Community Fellowship Church. The next step will be to establish long-term commitments and initiate outreach from individuals and groups committed to living in a specific neighborhood. New Hope Church in Oakland, California, narrowed its outreach to a specific geographic region—with most of their members living within blocks of the church and intentionally reaching a particular housing project. Through their efforts a specific neighborhood was changed by church members dwelling among and ministering justice and compassion.

MINISTRY OF INSTITUTIONAL JUSTICE

As ministry develops in a neighborhood, those ministering will become increasingly aware of the systemic nature of injustice. Structural evil becomes more evident as we move out of our positions of privilege and wealth. In our ministries of justice and compassion, we need to understand that the household of God is not merely called to provide simple solutions but to prophetically proclaim the justice of God. The geography of evil (i.e., the work of Satan on a systemic level) requires a response in kind.[5] Social injustice and systemic evil require a systemic response of biblical justice by the people of God.

A significant locus of systemic injustice is racism. Asian Americans have been conspicuously absent in the race dialogue in the United States. During the time of apartheid in South Africa, a special designation was created for Asian businessmen. Since Asians did not qualify as whites, nor would they want to be categorized as blacks or "coloreds," a special designation was created, "honorary white people."

America's original sin is the sin of racism. Racism led to the enslavement of Africans, the genocide of the Native Americans and the internment of Japanese Americans during World War II. Racism in some form or another has touched every ethnic minority group in the United States. And Asian Americans have even faced racist attitudes in the church. In the summer of 2004, for example, LifeWay Christian Resources (the publishing arm of the Southern Baptist Convention) produced vacation Bible school study material with the theme "Rickshaw Rally: Far Out, Far East." Under the auspices of promoting Japanese-themed VBS curriculum, LifeWay—tapping into stereotypical images—caricatured and generalized all Asian cultures. A significant number of Asian Americans informed LifeWay about the insensitive nature of this curriculum. But instead of pulling or changing the original material, LifeWay chose to ignore the concerns of the Asian American community. There were times in the history of race relations in America that the Asian American community tried to become honorary white people. Today we know that a clear and distinct voice needs to emerge from the Asian American community regarding the issue of race.

When we deal with issues of systemic injustice, one of the most significant areas of institutional social injustice is racial injustice. Given the sensitive nature of race, why did LifeWay and the Southern Baptists consistently ignore the Asian American voices of protest? Because they could. Asians are not only seen as the model minority, we are also seen as a silent minority. In effect, the Asian American Christian community in the United States has become the silent "model" minority community. Not only on issues of race but in other matters of structural injustice, Asians are seen but not heard.

Asian culture tends to shy away from confrontation. When faced with institutional injustice, confrontation is sometimes necessary. A collective voice addressing issues of systemic evil reflects a deepening concern for social justice ministry. While ministering to the immediate needs of the poor can yield short-term results, seeking long-term solutions usually involves addressing social injustice on a systemic and structural level. Will the emerging Asian American church be willing to confront issues such as poverty and racism?

The Complexity of Justice and Compassion Ministry

Kenny was eleven years old when I first met him. His family lived in the low-income apartment complex adjacent to the church. He showed up to the very first vacation Bible school we held, bringing all of his siblings and friends. Kenny was an affable and friendly kid, a real charmer. He would stop by my office just to chat. We'd talk about how he was doing in school and how his little brother and sisters were getting on his nerves. When the church was vandalized by another teenager from the neighborhood, Kenny came by to help clean up. When Kenny was too old to come to VBS as a student, he became a junior counselor.

Over the years Kenny grew taller and bigger, and he came to our children's programs less and less. His "big brother" from the church moved to another city. About a year ago, I noticed that he was wearing a red bandana. Then I'd see him in a red shirt and baggy pants with the red bandana over his head. Before, he'd go out of his way to say hi to me. Now he would nod silently in my direction or worse, he'd go out of his way to avoid me—especially when he was with his friends. His little brother told me that he was smoking pot. He was walking around the neighborhood when he should have been in school. I should have talked to him, taken him to see a movie, hung out with him more. But the church was growing. My family was growing. I had to spend more time supervising my church staff, thinking of ways to support our lay leadership, attending out-of-town conferences to speak glowingly about our urban-ministry programs. There didn't seem to be time. A neighborhood mom stopped to talk to me on the street. She said that I should talk to Kenny and his mother. Kenny was recently detained by the Department of Youth Services. His name is in the system now. I assured this mom that I would try to talk to Kenny as soon as possible. That was two weeks ago.

■   ■   ■

The ministry of the household of God is not a short-term pursuit. If God is calling the emerging Asian American church to exhibit the characteristics and values of the household of God, then that call will require a long-term commitment to justice and compassion ministries. Because of our immigrant experience, there are numerous obstacles for establishing healthy households of God within the Asian American Christian community. Being the church is a difficult calling, and striving to exhibit God's justice and compassion adds complexity to that calling.

Asian culture has a fairly narrow definition of success, which it values highly. Hence, the pressure to go to Harvard, to become an engineer or medical doctor and to live in a five-bedroom house with a three-car garage. Hence, the pressure to build larger and bigger churches with larger and bigger buildings. But striving to become the household of God may mean sacrificing these worldly measures of success. A church that seeks to exhibit justice and compassion may experience more failure than success.

After Christ established the church at the cost of his own life, he entrusted his church to human hands. We don't have the wisdom to question Jesus' choice in this matter. But if we trust Jesus' wisdom in placing his name upon us, we can trust that his Spirit is more than able to compensate for our deficiencies and is able to lead us as we embody the household of God.

During my first year in seminary I was full of dreams and wishes for future ministry. As I shared my grandiose plans with an older seminary student, I was surprised by his reply. He said that he envied my visions and dreams, but for various reasons he didn't particularly have grandiose visions of his own. In fact, his only desire was to be faithful to the Lord. May we hold on to the grand vision of God's calling to live out his justice and righteousness, but may we first and foremost be faithful to the Lord.

CONCLUSION

Measuring the Health of Our Households

S. STEVE KANG

HOW DO WE MEASURE THE HEALTH OF A CHURCH? Should we employ such diagnostics as the average worship attendance, the size of membership, the budget, the number of ministries or the size of the church staff? One wise Christian cultural critic recently suggested that the church should instead consider measures such as the percentage of active giving units in the church, the percentage of the budget set aside for the ministries outside of the local church, and the percentage of persons of color in the church. How do the former measures differ from the more specific measures the critic suggested? The latter measures are more specifically based on the ministry vision of the church and how well the church is carrying out the vision it's striving for.

However, even if we employ a set of quantifiable criteria to measure the health of the church based on its vision, it's hard to ascertain whether those measures truly reflect the breadth and depth of the health of the church. We have to admit that, having lived in the modern age, we have become increasingly dependent on "hard," or quantifiable, data to pinpoint objective, behavioral results. Meanwhile we forget to assess the "soft" data, or the issues of the heart—that is, motivations, feelings, longings and stories—that testify to the breadth and depth of our experiences.

Over the past three years and under the direction of the Catalyst Leadership Center, Asian American pastors and church leaders, sharing from their personal journeys and ministry experiences, tried to identify specific themes and ministries that contribute to the health of Asian American churches.[1] Instead of simply addressing commonly recognized aspects of the church—worship, proclamation, teaching, fellowship, service and stewardship—from an Asian American perspective, this book, which came out of the Catalyst forum, has sought to discuss nine salient values that integrate all of the functions of the church and promote spiritually healthy congregations.

THE NEXUS OF THE HOUSEHOLD OF GOD: GRACE AND TRUTH

We firmly believe that healthy Asian American churches must be reminded that the triune God has graciously invited his people to commune with him for eternity, and it is solely based on God's gracious election of his people through the life and work of Jesus Christ that we are given faith and called to be the household of God. For that reason the grace of God must pervade every aspect of our lives, challenging the sinful patterns and cultural norms that detract us from living as the household of God. Through word and deed, healthy Asian American churches proclaim the grace of God to one another and to the world. Grace-based Asian American churches create safe and hospitable places for the people of God to intentionally, habitually, and holistically engage one another as brothers and sisters in the household of God.

In John 1:14 the glory of God is said to be perfectly manifested in Jesus Christ, who is full of grace and truth. And in the following verses we are reminded that we have received that same grace and truth through Jesus Christ. God's grace and truth are demonstrated by the living Word in all he did and said, and are exemplified especially in his humiliation and humility to make visible the invisible God. As the people of God who have been elected in Jesus Christ from the foundation of the world, we are also called to exemplify through word and deed God's grace and truth in every aspect of the household of God.

Healthy Asian American churches see themselves as a truth-embodying community; the Bible permeates the very fabric of all that they do and say; God's Word masters them rather than they mastering it. These churches study and obey the Word of God, not merely to apply biblical principles to their lives but to enter, indwell and linger in God's redemptive drama. This requires that the household of God engages in deliberate historical and global reading of the Bible in the crucible of its local church context.

THE STEWARDS OF THE HOUSEHOLDS OF GOD

Healthy Asian American churches require a kind of leadership that strengthens the fabric of the household of God. The telos of such a leadership is not to merely obtain peak efficiency in the church, experiencing numerical growth in numbers, programs and financial strength, but to become more unified and cohesive in living out its God-given vision. Healthy Asian American churches know that many models of leadership are shaped more by the culture than by Christ. Thus their leaders must commit to genuine servanthood, exemplified in the radical humility of Jesus. Being a servant means that the leader is called to participate not only in Christ's resurrection but also in his sufferings and death. The apostle Paul reminds us that God wants church leaders to minister *through* their weaknesses and shortcomings. When we are weak, God is strong. Leaders of healthy Asian American churches must heed Paul's reminder in 2 Corinthians 4:15, 17-18:

> All this [suffering] is for your benefit, so that the grace that is reaching more and more people may cause thanksgiving to overflow to the glory of God. . . .
>
> For our light and momentary troubles are achieving for us an eternal glory that far outweighs them all. So we fix our eyes not on what is seen, but on what is unseen, since what is seen is temporary, but what is unseen is eternal.

Such weakness produces personal humility and brings a deeper understanding and fuller embrace of God's grace and of the hope of glory. Only when leaders understand that God alone has chosen them to lead and has endowed them with weaknesses as well as strengths, can they become servants rooted in the unmistakable character, sovereignty and promises of the triune God.

One hallmark of such Asian American church leaders is openness to change. For many, change does not come easily. Pastors and leaders of healthy Asian American churches, however, welcome change as God's initiative to transform us into the image of Jesus Christ. These leaders are poised to live and serve on the leading edge. Change creates pivot points or fertile moments in which God reveals his plan through and for the household of God.

Healthy Asian American churches understand that change for the sake of change or for the sake of duplicating another church's success does not accomplish God's purposes; rather, these churches are committed to understanding their own context and unique role in realizing God's kingdom in this world. One critical reminder is that, in advancing his eternal purposes, God alone forges new visions, directions and models of churches, even beyond this generation's aspirations and dreams. Toward that end, healthy Asian American churches must cultivate "active passivity" by waiting on the Lord while actively preparing themselves to follow him when the time comes.

Evangelism is a way of life for healthy Asian American churches. Evangelism is not seen as solely the responsibility of individual believers but as the very fabric of the household of God. Just as missions is integrated into every aspect of the missional church, healthy Asian American churches let the good news of Jesus Christ, the evangel, pervade every aspect of the church. Reclaiming the heritage of the early church, they focus on existing relationships within their communities, inducing friends and neighbors to consider life in the household of God. This "come and see" approach seeks to embody God's grace and truth through building long-term relationships. Healthy Asian American churches do not necessarily abandon traditional (modern) approaches to evangelism but seek to incorporate appropriate and often blended approaches that are uniquely suitable for postmodern Asian Americans. Rather than using shame or guilt to induce conversions, healthy Asian American churches rely on the Holy Spirit, who alone can bring about changes in hearts and souls for Christ.

As Jesus Christ affirmed in the high-priestly prayer in John's Gospel, the Father, Son and Holy Spirit are in perfect communion. Imaging the triune God, the unity of the people of God is one of the most compelling witnesses of Jesus Christ to the world. Through his death on the cross, Jesus Christ *has already* broken down the dividing wall of hostility. In light of what the Savior has accomplished, the household of God is called to appropriate this new reality. Healthy Asian American churches take the work of reconciliation seriously. For instance, rather than seeking autonomy through divisions along generational lines, healthy Asian American churches seek to maintain and strengthen intergenerational ties whenever possible. Such a partnership is a rewarding experience and honors God, testifying in a compelling manner to God's grace. Such partnership, however, is costly, requiring long-term commitments and sacrifice from both first- and second-generation congregations.

What about those Asian American churches that started with a vision to reach one generation of Asian Americans? Are they immune from building healthy intergenerational partnerships? By no means! Although they may take on different forms, building intergenerational partnerships is of utmost importance for these churches. Most of the Catalyst forum participants who have experienced both multigenerational and monogenerational churches agree that monogenerational Asian American churches who wish to grow should explore ways to creatively cultivate intergenerational and interdependent relationships with other healthy Asian American churches. These churches should seek possible intergenerational mentoring relationships and multigenerational ministry opportunities that mutually benefit and further strengthen the people and the churches involved.

Just as healthy intergenerational relationships within and among churches testify to the power of God to unite his people, so do healthy gender relations within the church. Healthy Asian American churches look afresh at how Christian men and women can live together as the household of God that reflects the perfect communion of the triune Godhead. As truth-embodying communities, these churches must not only examine the biblical texts that specifically address gender issues but also how differing herme-neutical traditions contribute to divergent understandings of those texts. Moreover, healthy Asian American churches should also interrogate any cultural and societal bias that might hinder both genders, but especially women, from building up the household of God through the exercise of spiritual gifts. Churches should be committed to rectifying or disbanding so-cioculturally shaped church practices, whether conscious or unconscious, that privilege males. Furthermore, recognizing the unfortunate social reality of gender inequality in society, healthy Asian American churches ought to address the particular needs of women, taking the initiative in empowering and affirming women as coheirs in Christ.

Healthy Asian American churches are increasingly cognizant of the need to engage in mercy and justice ministry in the church, the neighborhood and society at large. In line with its evangelical heritage, the Asian American church has, by and large, neglected the poor and marginalized of the society. Healthy Asian American churches take the commands of Jesus Christ seriously by becoming the bearers of his justice and mercy. These churches are not only informed about the plight of the marginalized and the need for biblical justice, but they are open to being transformed by the Holy Spirit, growing in compassion and ministering justice and mercy The participants in the Catalyst forum found that a key to a justice and mercy ministry is authentic and reciprocal partnerships with those whom the church is called to serve. Such a transformation is ultimately authenticated as the church's identity and mission is reshape through these efforts.

Growing healthy Asian American churches that embody God's grace and truth does not happen overnight. It involves a continuing acceptance of God's gracious invitation to enter, dwell and linger in the kingdom reality. As a part of God's mosaic of the saints from all times and places, the Asian American church must be faithful to its God-given vision and values, which are uniquely shaped in the crucible of God's redemptive history.

First, since the Asian American church is a relatively young church and does not share some of the history in American Protestantism, we seldom identify ourselves in rebellion or reaction against certain theological controversies within the church. Thus, we can be more fair-minded and judicious in assessing some of the painfully divisive issues and appreciating differing factions. Similarly, due to our experience as an ethnic minority in America, as well as in the American church, we are well poised to decipher the multiplicity of factors that inevitably often negatively influence the mission of the church in the world. For that reason, the Asian American church possesses the potential to take on an integral part in bringing reconciliation and forging working relationships across various dividing lines that exist in the American church. We are called to envision ourselves as mere catalysts in bringing further mending of the greater household of God in America and in the world.

Second, despite the inevitable tendency toward specialization and fragmentations in the (post) modern world and in the ministry of the church in particular, the Asian American church possesses a unique ethos and commitment to fostering a biblically based holism—that is functioning as a body, as a household of God. Having experienced a painful division between the immigrant generation and the subsequent generations of the Asian American church, it is vigilant against any sociocultural trends—based on class, gender, age groups, interests, etc.—that further divide the church. Instead, we are committed to the corporate lifestyle of the household of God that is characterized by mutual edification and mutual submission to one another. We are called to be witnesses to the world of how the unity and love of the Triune God has transformed and continues to transform our lives.

Last, although many Asian American Christians are well assimilated into mainstream America and into mainstream American churches, due mostly to our skin color among other salient distinguishing features, we will continue to face the predicament of being *the other* in the land we call home. Yet it is precisely for this reason that we are reminded in a more profound manner that we are to be aliens and strangers in this world, and that this world is not our home. We are called to be kingdom citizens and our true identity is found in no one else, except in Jesus Christ. In this sensate day and age, we are called to be the household of God in grace and truth that lives out the unmistakable kingdom reality, calling forth the American church to join God's eternal kingdom in this life. May growing Asian American churches respond to God's clarion call in this generation. *Soli Deo Gloria.*

CONTRIBUTORS AND
CATALYST FORUM PARTICIPANTS

CONTRIBUTORS

Peter Cha is associate professor of pastoral theology at Trinity Evangelical Divinity School in Deerfield, Illinois. He received his graduate training in theology from Trinity Evangelical Divinity School (M.Div. and Th.M), and received his doctorate in religion in society and personality from Northwestern University. He has previously served as a campus staff member with InterVarsity Christian Fellowship, as a youth pastor, and as a church planter and senior pastor. His publications include chapters in *Following Jesus Without Dishonoring Your Parents* (InterVarsity Press), articles in *Korean Americans and Their Religions* (Pennsylvania State University Press) and in *Telling the Truth: Evangelizing Postmoderns* (Zondervan), and articles in several scholarly and denominational journals.

S. Steve Kang is associate professor of educational ministries at Gordon-Conwell Theological Seminary, South Hamilton, Massachusetts. He previously served as associate professor of Christian formation and ministry and coordinator of interdisciplinary studies at Wheaton College in Illinois. His graduate training is in the areas of theology and religious education from Trinity Evangelical Divinity School, and he received his doctorate in religion in society and personality from Northwestern University. He has pastoral ministry experiences with youth, young adults and families, and in church planting. He has contributed to *Ex Auditu, Christian Education Journal* and *Religious Education Journal*. He is the author of *Unveiling the Socioculturally Constructed Multivoiced Self* (University Press of America). He is a coauthor of *A Many Colored Kingdom: Multicultural Dynamics for Spiritual Formation* (Baker).

Paul Y. Kim is a graduate of the University of Illinois, where he majored in electrical engineering. He has since dedicated himself to the reconciliation of and partnership between various generations of Korean Americans within a local church context. For the past fourteen years he has served as the senior pastor of Open Door Presbyterian Church in the metro D.C. area, which is nationally known as being one of the few that has successfully implemented a healthy partnership between the older immigrants and younger American-born congregants. As a result, Rev. Kim has become a renowned speaker and consultant on the topic of developing intergenerational relationships in ethnic churches. He also has a strong passion for missions and regularly accompanies members of his congregations to various points overseas. In addition to his B.S. from Illinois, he has both an M.Div. and a Th.M. from Trinity Evangelical Divinity School. He has also been serving as vice chairperson for Operation Mobilization Korean American Mission and as a member of the Catalyst Leadership Center board.

Dihan Lee serves as the associate English congregation pastor of Open Door Presbyterian Church. He works primarily with college-age students, but is also involved with men's ministry, the creative arts ministry and preaching. Dihan graduated from Northwestern University (1998) and attended Trinity Evangelical Divinity School (2001), where he received his M.Div. degree. After interning at NewSong Church in Southern California, he came to Open Door Presbyterian Church and is now in his second year of ministry. He has played an integral role in helping to develop the intergenerational ministry at Open Door Presbyterian Church.

Helen Lee is a freelance writer and consultant, with professional experiences in business, publishing and Christian ministry. She previously served as the associate director of the Best Christian Workplaces Institute (BCWI), an organization she cofounded in 2002. BCWI conducts the annual Best Christian Places to Work survey, the results of which are published in *Christianity Today* each spring. In addition to being a former editor and writer with *Christianity Today*, Helen has also worked with *re:generation quarterly* and as a campus staff worker with InterVarsity Christian Fellowship, where she pioneered the organization's first Asian American small group Bible study. She has also written about ethnic identity and faith issues in numerous publications. Helen attended Williams College, where she received a B.A.; Wheaton College, M.A.; and Babson College, M.B.A.

Grace May is currently teaching world Christianity at Gordon-Conwell Theological Seminary. Ordained in the Presbyterian Church (USA), she pastored at the Chinese Christian Church of New England and prior to that served at the African American Roxbury Presbyterian Church. Through her upbringing, travels and missions endeavors she has experienced a rich and varied sense of Christian community. Grace has contributed to *The Global God: Multicultural Evangelical Views of God*, *The IVP Women's Bible Commentary* and Christians for Biblical Equality's *Priscilla Papers*. Grace received her B.A. in English at Yale University, M.Div. at Gordon-Conwell Theological Seminary and Th.D. in theology and missiology at Boston University School of Theology.

Soong-Chan Rah is the founding and current senior pastor of the Cambridge Community Fellowship Church, a postmodern, multiethnic, urban church in the Central Square neighborhood of Cambridge, Massachusetts. Soong-Chan has previously been part of a church planting team in the Washington, D.C., area and worked as a campus staff worker with InterVarsity Christian Fellowship at MIT. He has preached in numerous crosscultural settings in churches and on college campuses, and was a plenary speaker at the Urbana 03 Student Mission Convention. Soong-Chan received his B.A.

in political science and history/sociology from Columbia University; his M.Div. from Gordon-Conwell Theological Seminary; his Th.M. from Harvard University; and his D.Min. from Gordon-Conwell Theological Seminary's Center for Urban Ministerial Education.

Nancy Sugikawa graduated from the University of California, Berkeley, with a B.S. in mechanical engineering. After working in the aerospace industry for a number of years, Nancy left engineering to join the pastoral staff of a multiethnic church plant in Sunnyvale, California. She then moved to southern California to complete her M.Div. degree from Fuller Theological Seminary in Pasadena. Nancy served as an associate pastor at NewSong Church in Irvine for four years, overseeing assimilation, evangelism and the ministry serving teams. She recently joined the pastoral staff of Lighthouse Christian Church in Issaquah, Washington, serving as consulting pastor in the areas of leadership and ministry development.

Jonathan Wu is executive pastor of Evergreen Baptist Church of Los Angeles. He previously served as the outreach pastor and has been on staff there for eleven years. He is a native of Chicago, graduating from Wheaton College and Trinity Evangelical Divinity School. He served with InterVarsity Christian Fellowship as a campus staff worker for nearly nine years. He is on the board of Catalyst Leadership Center. He is halfway through the D.Min. program at Fuller Theological Seminary.

Steve Wong is the founding and lead pastor of Grace Community Covenant Church, which he launched in 1998 to reach Asian Americans in Silicon Valley. He has spent more than twenty years in ministry. Steve previously worked in the Chinese church context as a youth pastor at Sunset Chinese Baptist Church in San Francisco and also as an associate pastor at San Jose Chinese Alliance Church. He received his M.Div. from Talbot School of Theology and also has a Ph.D. from The Center for Psychological Studies in Albany, California. Steve is a member of the executive board of the Pacific

Southwest Conference of the Evangelical Covenant Church and chairs the conference's Multiethnic Ministries Commission.

CATALYST FORUM PARTICIPANTS

David Gibbons has a passion for catalytic leadership development, church planting and community transformation. He is a graduate with honors from Dallas Theological Seminary, where he earned his Th.M. in 1989. In the late 1990s, *Christianity Today* recognized David as one of a new generation of evangelical leaders under forty. He has also been selected to participate in other "outside the box" leadership development programs such as Max DePree's Roundtable (he was one of only twelve selected for this national program) and Leighton Ford's Arrow Leadership Program. David was one of the founders of the Catalyst Leadership Center in 1991, and he subsequently launched and leads NewSong Church, one of the largest postmodern, multiethnic, multi-Asian churches in America. Currently David's focus is on developing new church multiplication models and arts centers, and on transforming communities in underresourced areas of the world. He also serves on the board of Catalyst Leadership Center.

Ken Fong is the senior pastor of Evergreen Baptist Church of Los Angeles, a congregation with the vision to foster a fresh model of a church for the next century, one that will be multi-Asian, multiethnic and multigenerational, and that offers Christ's real hope to real people. As of January 2005 the congregation averaged around seven hundred attendees of all ages and life stages, and includes first through fourth generations Asian Americans, with people from more than a dozen API groups plus a widening variety of non-APIs. Ken received his B.A. from the University of California, Berkeley, his M.Div. from American Baptist Seminary of the West and his D.Min. from Fuller Theological Seminary. His doctoral dissertation, "Insights for Growing Asian American Ministries," became a widely referenced text on the subject of contextualizing Asian culture within ministry. In November 1999

Judson Press published his reworked dissertation as *Pursuing the Pearl: A Comprehensive Resource for Multi-Asian Ministry.* InterVarsity Press published his second book, *Secure in God's Embrace: Living as the Father's Adopted Child* (2003). Ken was one of the original board members for IWA, a Christian nonprofit established to create more effective evangelistic tools to reach Japanese and Asian Americans. He also served as a trustee for InterVarsity Christian Fellowship from 1990-1994 and from 1997-2002. Since 1991 Ken has volunteered on a monthly basis at the Asian American Drug Abuse Program in Los Angeles and became a board member in 2001. That same year he became a contributing editor to Christianity Today's *Leadership Journal.* In 2002 Ken also became a trustee of Westmont College in Santa Barbara, California, and joined the advisory boards of the L2 Foundation (promoting Asian American Christian legacy-making and leadership development) and Emerging Ministries (Bay Area group that identifies, mentors and supports outstanding young local ministry entrepreneurs). His passion continues to burn for the forging of ministry approaches that are culturally attuned to reaching the hearts of Americanized Asian Americans, especially the unconvinced and the overlooked.

Wayne Ogimachi is a graduate of UCLA and Fuller Theological Seminary in the Los Angeles area, where he was raised. After involvement in youth, campus and pastoral ministry in southern California, he served the next seventeen years as the pastor of Christian Layman Church in Oakland, California. During those years he helped start the Asian American Christian Fellowship at the University of California, Berkeley, and spoke at many conferences and retreats. In the year 2000, Wayne moved to the Seattle area to become the founding pastor of Lighthouse Christian Church, a new ministry in Bellevue, Washington. He is on the board of directors of IWA and has contributed to articles in *Leadership* and *Building Church Leaders.*

Paul Tokunaga has worked with InterVarsity Christian Fellowship since 1973 in a variety of leadership and management roles. Currently, he serves as National Asian American Ministry Coordinator. He is a coauthor of *Following Jesus Without Dishonoring Your Parents* (1998), editor and coauthor of *Faith on the Edge* (1999), author of *The Power of Friendship* (2002) and *Invitation to Lead: Guidance for Emerging Asian American Leaders* (2003), all published by InterVarsity Press. He also edited *Developing Asian American Leaders* (1998), an in-house handbook for InterVarsity Christian Fellowship staff working with Asian American student leaders. He has written many articles for Christian and secular publications. Paul attended California Polytechnic State University, San Luis Obispo, receiving a B.S. in journalism, and New College Berkeley, receiving a Master of Christian Studies. Paul speaks regularly at conferences for adults and young professionals as well as for college students. He was a featured speaker at the Urbana 90 Student Mission Convention. He is also currently the director of The Daniel Project, a fifteen-month intensive leadership development program to prepare Asian Americans for senior leadership positions in InterVarsity Christian Fellowship.

NOTES

Chapter 1: Grace-Filled Households

[1]Paul Hiebert, "The Category 'Christian' in the Mission Task," *International Review of Mission* 72 (1983): 424.

[2]Russell Jeung, *Faithful Generations: Race and New Asian American Churches* (New Brunswick, N.J.: Rutgers University Press, 2005). This book contains a valuable analysis of the notion of "Asian American" in American society and American evangelicalism (see chapter one, pp. 1-15, and chapter four, pp. 63-81). Jeung included material interests and structural inequalities, as well as primordial values, as factors which contribute to a symbolic racial identity. He notes that the evangelical construct of "Asian American" focuses on factors that assist in personal evangelism, overlooking institutional and governmental factors. The result is an individualistic perspective that endorses racialization. A critique of this perspective is the subject of Michael O. Emerson and Christian Smith's book *Divided by Faith: Evangelical Religion and the Problem of Race in America* (New York: Oxford University Press, 2000).

Chapter 2: Truth-Embodying Households

[1]*Habitus,* or simply habit, is a disposition or state of the human being that involves the appetites, desires, affections, intellect, imagination, intuition, aesthetic sense, reason, conscience and will.

[2]Donald Bloesch, quoted in *The Christian Educator's Handbook on Spiritual Formation,* ed. Kenneth Gangel and James Wilhoit (Wheaton, Ill.: Victor Books, 1994), p. 45.

[3]Simon Chan, Ellen Charry, Marva Dawn and the late Stanley Grenz, among others.

[4]Ellen Charry, *Inquiring After God* (Oxford: Blackwell, 2000), p. xxiii.

[5]Ibid., p. xxii.

[6]Ken Fong, *Pursuing the Pearl* (Valley Forge, Penn.: Judson Press, 1999), p. 132.

[7]Kevin Vanhoozer, "'But That's Your Interpretation': Realism, Reading, and Reformation," *Modern Reformation,* July-August 1999, p. 27.

[8]Christopher Hall, *Reading Scripture with the Church Fathers* (Downers Grove, Ill.: InterVarsity Press, 1998), p. 42.

[9]Bruce McCormack, "Historical Criticism and Dogmatic Interest in Karl Barth's Theological Exegesis of the New Testament," in *Biblical Hermeneutics in Historical Perspective,* ed. Mark Burrows and Paul Rorem (Grand Rapids: Eerdmans, 1991), p. 338.

Chapter 3: Healthy Leaders, Healthy Households 1

[1]Max DePree, *Leadership Is an Art* (New York: Dell, 1989), p. 12.

[2]John Stott, *Basic Christian Leadership* (Downers Grove, Ill.: InterVarsity Press, 2002), p. 113.

[3]Myungseon Oh, "Study on Appropriate Leadership Pattern for the Korean Church in Post-modern Era," *Journal of Asian Mission* 5, no. 1 (2003): 132.

[4]Ibid.

[5]Karen J. Chai, "Competing for the Second Generation," in *Gatherings in Diaspora: Religious Communities and the New Immigration,* ed. R. Stephen Warner and Judith Wittner (Philadel-phia: Temple University Press, 1998), p. 299.

[6]E. Glenn Wagner, *Escape from Church, Inc.* (Grand Rapids: Zondervan, 1999), p. 104.

[7]Lewis B. Smedes, *Shame and Grace* (Grand Rapids: Zondervan, 1993), pp. 9-10.

[8]Christine J. Yeh and Karen Huang, "The Collectivistic Nature of Ethnic Identity Development Among Asian American College Students," *Adolescence*, September 1, 1996.

[9]Ibid.

[10]Ibid.

[11]Smedes, *Shame and Grace,* p. 38. Smedes continues by describing common sources of unde-served shame, which includes unaccepting parents, a topic which is probably of great rele-vance for Asian American leaders and is recommended for further reading.

[12]Paul Tokunaga, *Invitation to Lead* (Downers Grove, Ill.: InterVarsity Press, 2003), pp. 42-43. Tokunaga also provides guidance to help people determine whether the shame they are ex-periencing is healthy or unhealthy ("toxic"). For those who have questions regarding this topic, Tokunaga's book is well worth reading.

[13]Henri Nouwen, *In the Name of Jesus* (New York: Crossroad, 1992), pp. 63-64.

Chapter 4: Healthy Leaders, Healthy Households 2

[1]Henri Nouwen, *In the Name of Jesus* (New York: Crossroad, 1992), pp. 40, 41.

[2]It can also take a significant amount of time for a team of leaders to figure out how to work well together. But when it's clear there are problems among leaders, Asian American con-gregations are no different from other Christian organizations who want to demonstrate charity in their relationships with one another, so it's often difficult to let go of a team mem-ber who does not fit the team. David Gibbons says that it is more detrimental to continue in that situation rather than making the hard choice to let a team member go, or to leave, when necessary. And the responsibility lies equally with the team member as well as the team leader. "Sometimes you just have to agree to disagree and go separate ways. That is a last resort, especially in a congregational context. If there is a difference in vision and val-ues, and you as a staff member are not growing, you should feel a sense of blessing to go somewhere where you can grow, assuming you have aired your grievances and have main-tained civility with your fellow leaders," he says. "Not everyone will have chemistry with everyone else."

Greg Yee has seen the fallout from a number of churches who have not adopted a prac-tice of being slow to hire and quick to fire, when necessary. He says, "I hear over and over again stories of people who are in the wrong place with misplaced gifts, and how there is no system in place where there is a trial period to help ensure the possibility of a healthy courtship between a church and a pastor. When things do not work out, it can really hijack a church."

[3]George Cladis, *Leading the Team-Based Church* (San Francisco: Jossey-Bass, 1999), p. 26.

[4]Peter Senge, *The Fifth Discipline: The Art and Practice of the Learning Organization* (New York: Doubleday, 1990), p. 249.

[5]For specific strategies in resolving conflict see Duane Elmer, *Cross-Cultural Conflict* (Downers Grove, Ill.: InterVarsity Press, 1993). Chapter five contains information on using mediation to resolve conflicts; chapter six explores the "one-down position" strategy, which is especially helpful for shame-based cultures, and chapter twelve offers detailed principles on managing conflict.

[6]Terry Fullam, "The View from Above," *Leadership Journal*, winter 1984, p. 13.

[7]Senge, *Fifth Discipline*, p. 218.

[8]Fullam, "The View from Above," p. 19.

[9]Ibid., p. 22.

[10]Cladis, *Leading the Team-Based Church*, p. 99.

[11]Nouwen, *In the Name of Jesus*, p. 57.

Chapter 5: Trusting Households

[1]Robert E. Quinn, *Deep Change* (San Francisco: Jossey-Bass, 1996), p. 24.

[2]Erwin McManus, *An Unstoppable Force* (Loveland, Colo.: Group, 2001), p. 81.

[3]Michael O. Emerson and Christian Smith, *Divided by Faith: Evangelical Religion and the Problem of Race in America* (New York: Oxford University Press, 2000).

[4]Quinn, *Deep Change*, p. 86.

[5]John Kotter, *Leading Change* (Boston: Harvard Business School Press, 1996), p. 162.

Chapter 6: Hospitable Households

[1]Ken Fong, *Secure in God's Embrace* (Downers Grove, Ill.: InterVarsity Press, 2003), p. 16.

[2]Robert Coleman, *The Master Plan of Evangelism* (Grand Rapids: Revell, 1991), pp. 33, 38.

[3]Although Jesus is the only one who can be fully incarnated in the lives of people as the God incarnate, we are called to testify to the God who is with us through our presence and obedience. Thanks to Steve Kang for his observation on this point.

[4]Ken Fong, *Pursuing the Pearl* (Valley Forge, Penn.: Judson Press, 1999), pp. 104, 114.

[5]Rick Richardson, *Evangelism Outside the Box* (Downers Grove, Ill.: InterVarsity Press, 2000), pp. 51-52.

[6]Ibid., p. 100.

[7]In *Pursuing the Pearl,* Fong writes about the ways that his church tried to convert its worship space—"a multipurpose building . . . that resembled a Costco warehouse store"—into a sanctuary designed to fit an Asian American congregation:

> Using what we considered to be a Japanese palette, we had the sanctuary painted a cool shade of gray, with the glossy black doorjambs framing doors of darker gray. The wall-to-wall carpet is an eggplant purple, and the interlocking, ergonomic, light-colored birch chairs are upholstered in a neutral blue-gray fabric.   . . . The temporary baptistery is off to one side, partially hidden by a tall, multipanelled Japanese *shoji* screen and plants. All eyes are naturally drawn to the prominent soffit with its front cutout in the shape of a cross. This overhang defines the pulpit area

and conveys the light from the skylight above onto the custom-designed, minimalist, light-colored, wooden pulpit. The stark simplicity of this focal point is striking. A beautiful satin banner festooned with crosses hangs in the open space in the pulpit's center. . . . To the best of our ability, given the limitations of our space and budget, we wanted to create a room where Asian Americans, especially postmodern-minded, unconvinced ones, would feel free to worship God.

[8]Fong, *Secure in God's Embrace,* p. 125.

[9]Richardson, *Evangelism Outside the Box,* p. 20.

Chapter 7: Multigenerational Households

[1]Min-ho Song, "Constructing a Local Theology for a Second-Generation Korean Ministry," *Urban Missions* 15 (1997): 28.

Chapter 8: Gender Relations in Healthy Households

[1]For a incisive treatment of gender relations at creation, read part one of Mary Stewart Van Leeuwen's *Gender and Grace* (Downers Grove, Ill.: InterVarsity Press, 1990).

[2]For a study of women leaders in the Bible leaders, see Mary B. Evans, *Woman in the Bible,* 2nd ed. (Carlisle, U.K.: Paternoster, 1998) and for an exegetical treatment of the difficult Pauline passages, see Craig Keener's *Paul, Women and Wives* (Peabody, Mass.: Hendrickson, 1992), and Aida B. Spencer's *Beyond the Curse: Women Called to Ministry* (Nashville: Thomas Nelson, 1985; reprint, Peabody, Mass.: Hendrickson, 1995). For a close examination of 1 Timothy 2, see Richard and Catherine Kroeger's *I Suffer Not a Woman* (Grand Rapids: Baker Books, 1992).

[3]Christians for Biblical Equality is an evangelical organization that supports the egalitarian view of women in ministry. See their website at <www.cbeinternational.org>.

[4]Council for Biblical Manhood and Womanhood is an evangelical organization that supports the complementarian view of women in ministry. See their website at <www.cbmw.org>.

[5]Paul Little, *Know Why You Believe* (Downers Grove, Ill.: InterVarsity Press, 1968).

[6]Rick Richardson, *Evangelism Outside the Box* (Downers Grove, Ill.: InterVarsity Press, 2000), pp. 30-40.

[7]Ken Fong, *Pursuing the Pearl* (Valley Forge, Penn.: Judson Press, 1999), p. 181.

[8]The following are some of the recently published resources that can be helpful to your study: Ronald Pierce and Rebecca Groothuis, eds., *Discovering Biblical Equality* (Downers Grove, Ill.: InterVarsity Press, 2004); John Piper and Wayne Grudem, eds., *Recovering Biblical Manhood and Womanhood* (Wheaton, Ill.: Crossway, 1991); Stanley Grenz and Denise Kjesbo, *Women in the Church* (Downers Grove, Ill.: InterVarsity Press, 1995); Aida B. Spencer, *Beyond the Curse: Women Called to Ministry* (Nashville: Thomas Nelson, 1985; reprint, Peabody, Mass.: Hendrickson, 1995); Elaine Storkey, *Origins of Difference: The Gender Debate Revisited* (Grand Rapids: Baker, 2001); Mary Stewart Van Leeuwen, *Gender and Grace* (Downers Grove, Ill.: InterVarsity Press, 1990); Sarah Sumner, *Men and Women in the Church: Building Consensus on Christian Leadership* (Downers Grove, Ill.: InterVarsity Press, 2003); and James Beck and Craig Blomberg, eds. *Two Views on Women in Ministry, Counterpoint* (Grand Rapids: Zondervan, 2001).

Chapter 9: Households of Mercy and Justice

[1]Glen H. Stassen and David P. Gushee, *Kingdom Ethics* (Downers Grove, Ill.: InterVarsity Press, 2003), p. 345.

[2]Jim Wallis, "The Second Reformation Has Begun," in *Envisioning the New City: A Reader on Urban Ministry,* ed. Eleanor Scott Meyers (Louisville, Ky.: Westminster John Knox, 1992), p. 58.

[3]Ibid., p. 59.

[4]John M. Perkins, *Restoring At-Risk Communities* (Grand Rapids: Baker Books, 1995), p. 22.

[5]Eldin Villafane, *Seek the Peace of the City* (Grand Rapids,: Eerdmans, 1995), p. 26.

Conclusion

[1]For more on Catalyst Leadership Center and the forum for Asian American church leaders, see pp. 12-13.